Contents

To see a world in a grain of sand
And a heaven in a wild flower,
Hold infinity in the palm of your hand
And eternity in an hour.

William Blake

Be regular and orderly in your life, so that you
may be violent and original in your work.

Gustave Flaubert

To sin by silence, when we should protest,
Makes cowards out of men.

Ella Wheeler Wilcox

For AP, who over the years has urged me
to write about Rachel Carson

PUFFIN BOOKS
Published by the Penguin Group
Penguin Young Readers Group, 345 Hudson Street, New York, New York 10014, U.S.A.
Penguin Group (Canada), 90 Eglinton Avenue East, Suite 700, Toronto, Ontario, Canada M4P 2Y3
(a division of Pearson Penguin Canada Inc.)
Penguin Books Ltd, 80 Strand, London WC2R 0RL, England
Penguin Ireland, 25 St Stephen's Green, Dublin 2, Ireland (a division of Penguin Books Ltd)
Penguin Group (Australia), 250 Camberwell Road, Camberwell, Victoria 3124, Australia
(a division of Pearson Australia Group Pty Ltd)
Penguin Books India Pvt Ltd, 11 Community Centre, Panchsheel Park, New Delhi - 110 017, India
Penguin Group (NZ), 67 Apollo Drive, Rosedale, North Shore 0632, New Zealand
(a division of Pearson New Zealand Ltd)
Penguin Books (South Africa) (Pty) Ltd, 24 Sturdee Avenue, Rosebank, Johannesburg 2196, South Africa

Registered Offices: Penguin Books Ltd, 80 Strand, London WC2R 0RL, England

First published in the United States of America by Viking, a division of Penguin Young Readers Group, 2007
Published by Puffin Books, a division of Penguin Young Readers Group, 2008

3 5 7 9 10 8 6 4 2

Text copyright © Ellen Levine, 2007
Photo credits can be found on page 218.
All rights reserved

LIBRARY OF CONGRESS CATALOGING-IN-PUBLICATION DATA IS AVAILABLE

Puffin Books ISBN 978-0-14-241046-2

Set in Goudy
Book design by Jim Hoover

Printed in the United States of America

Except in the United States of America, this book is sold subject to the condition
that it shall not, by way of trade or otherwise, be lent, re-sold, hired out, or otherwise
circulated without the publisher's prior consent in any form of binding or cover
other than that in which it is published and without a similar condition
including this condition being imposed on the subsequent purchaser.

The publisher does not have any control over and does not assume
any responsibility for author or third-party Web sites or their content.

UP*close:*

Rachel Carson

a twentieth-century life by
ELLEN LEVINE

PUFFIN BOOKS

READ ALL THE BOOKS IN THE
UP*close* SERIES

Determined

The research was massive; the work, monumental; that Rachel completed it in her condition, extraordinary. Her last task was to write the first chapter, "A Fable for Tomorrow." She wrote of a town "in the heart of America where all life seemed to live in harmony with its surroundings . . . Then a strange blight crept over the area and everything began to change." Death hovered over people as well as animals. Birds vanished; it was a "spring without voices." Streams were lifeless and roadside flowers withered. "No witchcraft, no enemy action had silenced the rebirth of a new life in this stricken world. The people had done it themselves." Rachel explained that no single town had experienced all these disasters, but every one of them had happened someplace. Without care, "this imagined tragedy may easily become a stark reality we all shall know."

Foreword

IN 1961, MY friend Micki wrote me that there were dozens of dead robins all over the University of Wisconsin campus. It was curious and frightening, she said. A year later, we both understood why these eagerly awaited birds of spring were dying in such great numbers. That year Rachel Carson's book *Silent Spring* was published. Carson sounded an alarm heard around the world: if we don't stop spraying our gardens and fields, forests and rivers with toxic pesticides, we will poison the environment and the creatures that live in it, including ourselves.

Probably many of you opening this book have never heard of Rachel Carson. Yet there was a time when the whole world knew her name. President Kennedy praised her; chemical corporations condemned her. Just after *Silent Spring* was published, I had dinner with my friend Karen and a guy she had started to date. He was a chemist with a big company. The conversation turned to Carson's new book, and he began to denounce both the book and author as ill-informed, hysterical, and inaccurate. Something prompted me to ask, "Have you read it?" He twisted his napkin. "No." Our laughter drowned out his explanations about knowing "anyhow" it was a bad book.

When the book first came out, *Time* magazine had called Carson's conclusions "patently unsound." Nearly forty years later, *Time* changed its mind. "Before there was an environmental movement," their article said, "there was one brave woman and her very brave book." The magazine then named her one of the one hundred most influential people of the twentieth century, along with Albert Einstein and Jonas Salk.

"Every once in a while in the history of mankind," one senator said, "a book has appeared which has substantially altered the course of history. . . . One can think of many examples, such as *Uncle Tom's Cabin*, for instance. [*Silent Spring*] is of that important character." When meeting Harriet Beecher Stowe, the author of *Uncle Tom's Cabin*, President Abraham Lincoln is reported to have said, "So you're the little woman who started this great war!" If Lincoln had been president in 1962, he might well have greeted Rachel Carson as the little woman who started the environmental revolution.

A year after *Silent Spring* was published, I was hired to work on a twelve-part public television series to be called *The Environmental Revolution*. At the time, Rachel Carson was very ill, but my colleague and I met with many of her scientist and naturalist friends. In the end, public television couldn't get the funding, and the programs were never made. But I've never forgotten my trip into Rachel's world of nature. I have her picture over my desk, and sometimes I actually think we've talked.

But why would *you* want to read about Rachel Carson? She wasn't the head of a government. She wasn't a millionaire. She wasn't a movie star or a brilliant athlete. But Rachel Carson *is* one of the few people who wrote a book that actually changed the world.

How did she get to be such a person? What made her curious to ask questions others shied away from? What made her fearless in the face of formidable enemies?

This is her story.

Rachel hiking on Cobb Island, Virgina, 1946.

Introduction

KLIEG LIGHTS BEAM on the stage of the White House press room. It's August 29, 1962, and newspaper, magazine, radio, and television reporters from the U.S. and around the world pack the room. The president, John F. Kennedy, is a year and a half into his term. He's smart, funny, assertive, and reflective by degrees at his press conferences. He is a president comfortable with reporters' questions.

And the reporters are ready. The *New Yorker* magazine recently published a three-part serialization of a book called *Silent Spring* by biologist Rachel Carson. The articles created a sensation even before the book's official publication date in September. No one was prepared for the extent of the public response and its intensity. Newspapers and magazines received letters by the score from readers deeply troubled by Carson's message that government and big business interests are turning a blind eye to the poisoning of the environment with toxic chemical pesticides.

New York Congressman John V. Lindsay read the final section of the first *New Yorker* installment into the *Congressional Record*. Letters poured into Congress, the U.S. Departments of Agriculture and Interior, the Federal Pest Control Review Board, the Public Health Service, and the Food and Drug Administration. State, county, and local government agencies were also besieged with questions.

What are you doing about this? the public demanded to know.

President Kennedy, a regular reader of the *New Yorker*, walks to the podium. Pads flip open, hands shoot up.

"Mr. President," a reporter calls out, "there appears to be a growing concern among scientists as to the possibility of dangerous long-range side effects from the use of DDT and other pesticides." The president listens attentively. "Have you considered," the reporter continues, "asking the Department of Agriculture or the Public Health Service to take a closer look at this?"

The president nods. "Yes, and I know that they already are." In the next moment, the world's most powerful political leader enters Rachel Carson's name into the history books. "I think particularly, of course," the president says, "since Miss Carson's book . . ."

Young Rachel

ONE
Wild Birds and Creatures

AS A CHILD, Rachel Carson yearned to see the ocean, but she was land bound. She grew up outside Pittsburgh, surrounded by woods and fields and a powerful curving river, the Allegheny. A child of the river, she dreamed of the ocean. Having never seen it, she pictured foam-crested waves and imagined the sounds of the pounding surf. Perhaps it was the fossilized fish she found in the cliffs behind the farm that inspired her wonder, or the conch shell on the mantelpiece, the kind that holds the memory of the ocean's roar in its spiral twist. In her own world, Rachel watched and listened to birds and small animals. She learned to "wear the skin" of other creatures, see life through their eyes.

How many people realize their dreams? Rachel was one of that lucky band. She became the preeminent "biographer" of the sea, and her writing helped save the natural world she so loved.

* * *

On May 27, 1907, Maria Carson described her newborn child Rachel as a "dear, plump, little blue-eyed baby," "unusually pretty" and "very good." Rachel's older sister Marian was in the fifth grade, and her brother Robert in first grade. Robert Carson Sr., a traveling sales representative for an insurance company, was often away from home. Maria Carson's older children weren't particularly interested in nature, but Rachel loved walking with her mother through fields and woods, smelling flowers and listening to bird songs. Mrs. Carson didn't teach her to memorize bird and plant and insect names. When you see creatures in the places they live, she would say, watch them as they go about their lives. Then their names will have meaning. And Rachel understood.

Rachel's mother, Maria McLean Carson, was born in 1869, the daughter of a Presbyterian minister. She was eleven when her father died. Maria, studious and bright, attended a finishing school for young Christian women and graduated in 1887 with honors in Latin and training in music. She became a schoolteacher and also gave private piano lessons. At a concert in the early 1890s, Maria sang with a local choral group. A good-looking, somewhat shy young man named Robert Carson was also on the program. He courted Maria, and a year later they were married. She was forced to give up her job, since married women at that time in Pennsylvania were not allowed to teach. Robert Carson didn't earn much money as a company clerk, but it was enough to start a family. Within a few years their daughter Marian and son Robert were born.

In 1900 Carson took out a loan and bought sixty-five acres of farmland and woods on a hillside in Springdale, a river town fifteen miles north of Pittsburgh. The property included a small two-story house, barn, outhouses, chicken coop, and springhouse. Maria Carson cooked in a lean-to kitchen attached to the back of the main house. There were always apples from an orchard up the hill, known as "Carson's Grove," where local residents often picnicked.

The house was a "two over two," two rooms downstairs on either side of a central staircase and two rooms above. The Carsons carried water from the springhouse built into the hillside some fifty feet away. For the thirty years Rachel's family lived in Springdale, there was no indoor plumbing. On cold winter days, the family sat in front of the fireplaces or a coal stove, and kept to a minimum any trips to the outhouse. In the heat of summer, Rachel and her sister and brother cooled off in the dirty Allegheny River.

Robert Carson did not see himself as a farmer. He had big dreams, and planned to divide his land into lots for sale. Pittsburgh, a town of steel mills and factories, was booming. The river and railroad were busy with traffic bringing in raw materials and taking away manufactured goods. Springdale, just up river, seemed to be in exactly the right spot to be part of that boom.

Robert Carson wasn't alone in his hopes for Springdale. The city's population doubled in the early part of the century, but then economic downturn ended his dream. Banks and businesses had several bad years, labor strikes disrupted factories, and Carson's real estate lots went unsold. The Panic of 1907 had spread economic trouble across the country. Rachel was born in the middle of this financial turmoil, and although the nation's fortunes recouped, the Carsons struggled.

Rachel, unaware of her family's problems, explored the fields and woods, brimming with life. She described herself as a "solitary child . . . happiest with wild birds and creatures as companions." "I can remember no time," she said, "when I wasn't interested in the out-of-doors and the whole world of nature."

Rachel's mother, like many people at the turn of the century, was an avid bird-watcher and a believer in the importance of nature study for young people. Mrs. Carson taught her daughter that we share the world with other creatures. Young Rachel watched her mother carry insects out of the house and release them. Years later, after looking through her microscope at starfish or ghost crabs or tiny snails she had collected from tide pools, Rachel would return them to their edge-of-the-sea home.

On an early fall morning in 1913, Maria Carson took Rachel to Springdale grammar school for her first day of school. She enjoyed school, but she spent many days at home. From second through seventh grades, if the weather was bitter cold or some illness was going around, Rachel stayed home and was taught by her mother. Mrs. Carson had reason to be afraid. Childhood diseases like diphtheria, scarlet fever, typhoid fever, and whooping cough were sometimes fatal. Unlike today, there were no antibiotics or flu shots. Polio in the first half of the twentieth century was one of the most dreaded diseases. In 1916 in New York City alone, more than 9,000 people died of polio complications, and over 27,000 were paralyzed, many of them children.

Rachel's second-grade teacher marked her "present" only sixteen days during the first three months of 1914. In fourth grade, Rachel was absent for a full month. But Mrs. Carson was a thorough teacher, and Rachel was usually an A student, even with her absences.

Rachel loved Beatrix Potter's stories and *The Wind in the Willows*. "I read a great deal almost from infancy," she said, "and I suppose I must have realized someone wrote the books, and thought it would be fun to make up stories, too." Rachel and her mother once brought home several baby robins after their nest had been destroyed. They made a home for the birds on the screened porch until they learned to fly. Perhaps Rachel thought of them when she wrote "The Little Brown House," a story about wrens searching for a home. In another tale, her rabbit character had a book called *Peter Rabbit* on his reading table.

Each month when *St. Nicholas* magazine arrived Rachel read it from cover to cover. Famous writers like Mark Twain and Louisa May Alcott contributed poems and stories, and Norman Rockwell's illustrations enlivened the pages. Founded in 1873, *St. Nicholas* was rated by many as the best magazine ever published for children.

Mary Mapes Dodge, the founding editor, had wanted the magazine to be a "child's playground; where children could be delighted as well as be in charge." The section of the magazine called the St. Nicholas League sponsored contests and printed children's writings and drawings. Winners were awarded gold badges, with silver badges for runners-up. Honor members, those who had won both silver and gold badges, received a cash prize.

By age ten, Rachel was ready to show the world her writing. On a September morning in 1918, she waited expectantly for the mail. Just before her eleventh birthday, she had submitted her first story to the League. As required, her mother had written in the upper corner of the paper, "this story was written without assistance, by my little ten-year-old daughter, Rachel." When the

September 1918 issue of the magazine arrived, there it was, "A Battle in the Clouds," with the byline "Rachel L. Carson." Best of all were the magic words "silver badge."

"I doubt that any royalty check of recent years has given me as great joy as the notice of that award," Rachel recalled. With her silver badge, Rachel was in extraordinary company. Seven years earlier, E. B. White, future author of *Charlotte's Web* and *Stuart Little* had also won a League silver badge. And there were other winners who became famous as adults—novelists William Faulkner and F. Scott Fitzgerald, and poets E. E. Cummings and Edna St. Vincent Millay.

Thrilled at seeing her story in print, Rachel sat down to write more. With the entry of the U.S. into World War I, her brother had enlisted. And so Rachel focused on war stories. In February 1919, she was awarded a gold badge. Now an honor member, having won both silver and gold, Rachel received a check for ten dollars, a royal sum in those days. By the end of the year she'd had four stories published. She knew with absolute certainty she wanted to be a writer.

Writing was also a way for Rachel to ignore the chaos

at home. Marian was more like a young aunt than an older sister. Anxious to be on her own, she had dropped out of school at the end of tenth grade to get a job. When Rachel was eight, Marian had rushed into a marriage. The young couple moved in with the Carsons, and for a few months before Robert Jr. enlisted, six people had slept in the four-room house. When her brother was discharged from the Army Air Service in 1919, he moved back into the crowded Springdale homestead.

Times were hard for the Carsons. They didn't consider themselves poor, but they were almost always short of cash. Mrs. Carson gave piano lessons for fifty cents a session to add to the family coffers. Rachel's father took a part-time job at West Penn Power Plant to supplement his income from selling insurance. And Robert Jr. and Marian also worked at the plant. West Penn Power, with its pollution-spewing chimney stacks, was at that time the primary source of income for the family of Rachel Carson, the future environmentalist who would so eloquently alert the world to the dangers of pollution.

Rachel graduated from eighth grade in 1921. That summer she wrote an essay about *St. Nicholas*. The magazine bought the piece to use in its advertising, and Rachel was paid a penny a word. If "turning pro" means getting paid (not as a prize) for your work, then that three-dollar check was the start of Rachel's career. She must have thought so, for she wrote "first payment" on the check envelope and never threw it out.

At fifteen, Rachel sent a story called "My Favorite Recreation" to the St. Nicholas League. It was her first nature writing, and told of a day's hike she took with her dog deep into the woods, looking for birds' nests.

Soon our trail turned aside into deeper woodland. It wound up a gently sloping hill, carpeted with fragrant pine-needles. It was our own discovery, Pal's and mine, and the fact gave us a thrill of exultation. . . .

Near at hand we heard the cheery "witchery, witchery," of the Maryland yellow-throat. For half an hour we trailed him, until we came out on a sunny slope. There in some low bushes we found the nest, containing four jewel-like eggs. To the little owner's consternation, we came close enough to snap a picture.

All her life Rachel was happiest when on similar excursions. In the pages of *St. Nicholas*, thousands of readers walked with her and Pal, as in later years many millions would explore with her the edge of the seashore and the ocean's blackest depths.

In the fall of 1922, most of Rachel's classmates traveled to different schools in the area, since Springdale did not have a four-year high school. Rachel's old school did offer classes for the first two years of high school, so she stayed home, attended those classes, and saved transportation costs.

For the last two years, Rachel traveled to Parnassus High School, only a few miles away by streetcar. By all accounts she enjoyed these years. She played basketball and hockey and cheered at pep rallies for the Parnassus football team. And she maintained a high grade-point average.

Her senior thesis was called "Intellectual Dissipation." In a tone both earnest and a bit heavy-handed, she challenged mental laziness, lest "we recklessly squander our natural resources." It's easy to quote from famous writers, she said, but we must use our own intellect, or we are "merely slavish imitators, mouthpieces for the thoughts of others." Her thesis reflected a strong sense of self that she would draw on when she came under fierce attack nearly forty years later. But Rachel also had a wry sense of humor. She drew sketches of classmates, and wrote "good-humored" limericks about each one.

Rachel graduated first in her class of twenty-eight girls and sixteen boys. Her parents took great pride in her achievement, particularly as it contrasted with the troubles of their older children. Robert was now living at the family homestead with a wife and baby; Marian, who had married again in 1921, had two children, Rachel's infant nieces Virginia and Marjorie. But Marian's second marriage was falling apart, an event that would alter Rachel's life in ways no one could have imagined.

Rachel, however, on that bright May morning of her graduation, was focused on a new adventure, college—a word and a world loaded with possibility.

TWO

The Vision Splendid

IT WAS ONLY sixteen miles from Springdale to Pennsylvania College for Women (PCW) in Pittsburgh, but when Rachel Carson arrived on campus, she had traveled to a new world. The school sat high on a hill overlooking downtown Pittsburgh, an oasis above the city's bustle. Its three main buildings were covered with ivy and surrounded by gardens.*

One thing, however, was familiar to Rachel. Pollution. Pittsburgh was one of dirtiest cities in the nation. Coal dust belched from factory smokestacks. But ash and grit refuse to stay within factory gates. Some days on campus the air was so thick with industrial smog, the sun was grayed over, and the smell of ash hung in the air.

Still, Rachel was thrilled to begin this new life. In an essay for freshman English composition, "Who I Am

* See Notes for additional information.

and Why I Came to P.C.W.," she described herself as a "girl of eighteen years, a Presbyterian, Scotch-Irish by ancestry, and a graduate of a small, but first class high school." This is straightforward, if not ordinary, but she wrote more, of wanting to do something of significance. "Sometimes I lose sight of my goal, then again it flashes into view, filling me with a new determination to keep the 'vision splendid' before my eyes. I may never come to a full realization of my dreams, but 'a man's reach must exceed his grasp, or what's a heaven for?'"

Unlike her mother's generation, young women like Rachel often went on to college. Even so, the emphasis was still on preparing graduates for marriage and motherhood. In between diaper-washing and cooking, it was assumed young women would read, pass on their interests to their children, and converse intelligently at the dinner table with their husbands. Before marriage they might teach or do clerical work. They were not expected to become doctors, lawyers, or scientists. Those were "male professions." PCW president Cora Coolidge, a supporter of higher education for women, was still a woman of her time. Her students received training in good grooming and proper social behavior, and attended regular social teas. Rachel and a friend went to one tea where stuffed avocado was served. Neither girl had ever tasted an avocado. When they walked out, Rachel said, "Well, I could really go for a nice big bread and jelly sandwich right now."

Mrs. Carson had never considered any school other than PCW for Rachel. It was a nondenominational Christian school close to home, had high academic standards, and offered scholarship aid. Tuition, room and board, books, and other fees came to about $1,000. Rachel received a $200 scholarship, but that wasn't enough. President Coolidge recognized Rachel's potential and arranged for private, unofficial assistance from wealthy friends of the college to make up the balance.

There were always other expenses—clothes, trips home, and the occasional ice-cream soda. Rachel, however, did not work part-time during the school year. Her mother wanted her to be a full-time student. Mrs. Carson, on the other hand, took on more piano students and sold some of the china and silver pieces she had inherited from her mother.

Many PCW students from wealthy homes in the Pittsburgh area had active social lives. This was, after all, the middle of the "roaring twenties." Rachel was different not only in her economic situation but in her interests. A high-school classmate thought her lucky to be near so many male students at Pittsburgh University and Carnegie Tech. Rachel quickly replied that she planned to major in literature, not boys. If she missed having fancy party dresses, she never said.

Mrs. Carson shared as much as she could of Rachel's new world. Many weekends she traveled to the college on a Saturday afternoon, read with Rachel in the library, typed her papers, and returned to Springdale that evening. It was a college experience, albeit vicarious, that Maria Carson must have always wanted. Several of Rachel's classmates disliked Mrs. Carson, who "'bragged on' Rachel ad nauseum." Some called her "the commuter," since she was so often on campus.

By the fall, Rachel was known as a bright student, a description not always guaranteed to win friends. She was never a part of the in-group; the popular crowd scorned her homemade clothes, her close relationship with her mother, and her concentration on her work.

Every school has its bullies, and Rachel was some-times the "girl on whom they played practical jokes, such as calling her to the phone when no one was there, putting cleaning powder in her bed, short sheeting it." After Rachel became famous, one classmate said "how much better her hair looked after professional care." Rachel's graduation picture in her class yearbook, however, is a portrait of a lovely-looking young woman, one of the most attractive in her class. So perhaps some of the mean-spirited tone was provoked by envy.

Rachel had entered PCW as a freshman steeped in the classics of English literature. She had read Shakespeare and Milton, and loved Dickens and Scott. Mark Twain was clearly her favorite American author. "His philosophy, humor, and straight-forward hatred of hypocrisy have touched a responsive chord in my heart." At the end of the first semester, Rachel was one of the top ten students in her class.

Rachel "wasn't anti-social," one student recalled. "She just wasn't social." And Rachel was on scholarship, "more of a stigma in those days." Another classmate described Rachel as "much more of a scholar than the rest of us and in a way withdrawn," but added, "she entered into things with great spirit. When you asked her to do something, she did it wholeheartedly—if she wanted to do it." And Rachel wanted to play sports. She went out for hockey and basketball. Short, slight, but plucky, she was a determined player. She made the teams as a substitute.

That first year Rachel found a mentor in Grace Croff, the assistant professor who taught freshman composition. Croff was faculty advisor to the student newspaper *The Arrow* and the literary supplement, *The Englicode*, and encouraged Rachel to write for both. Rachel's first submission to *The Englicode*, a short story called "The Master of the Ship's Light," was accepted for publication. We can see in it the beginning steps

Rachel (on right) at PCW with Professor Grace Croff.

of the writer who would become world-famous for her books about the sea. In her story, the ocean was as important a character as the people. Rachel wrote of "long lazy swells that rolled in on the shallow beach," "patches of white foam, betraying the menacing reefs beneath," "towering waves" beating on an inhospitable coast "with uncontrollable fury," and "the booming of the breakers resound[ing] for miles"—all images summoned from her imagination. *She herself had never seen the ocean.*

Rachel completed her first year at PCW believing she was on the road to her "vision splendid." She had written her first piece for the college's literary magazine, and she was one of the top students in her class.

PCW required all students to take a full year of science courses. At the start of sophomore year, Rachel signed up for two semesters of biology. Dorothy Thompson, one of Rachel's classmates in the biology course, initially saw Rachel as "so reserved and sober." She soon discovered that Rachel was actually quite friendly. During one lab session, Dorothy struggled, "trying to sketch a small protozoan so fast moving that it kept swimming into and out of focus in the drop of water under my microscope."

"Here's a good specimen to sketch," Rachel said, offering Dorothy her own slide. "My animal has slowed down and is easy to keep in focus."

"What I had judged as unfriendliness was self-containment," Dorothy remembered.

As an English major, Rachel had accepted without challenge the commonly held belief that there was a sharp distinction between literature and science. Art conveyed the beauty and meaning of life; science, on the other hand, was utilitarian, necessary as a practical matter.

Then Rachel met Mary Scott Skinker, the teacher of her biology class and acting head of the biology department. She was elegant, glamorous, and vivacious. Skinker's passion for the natural world matched Rachel's. Field trips to hillsides, creeks, riverbeds to see creatures in their natural environment were a grown-up version of Rachel's excursions at home. In her first college essay, Rachel had written, "I love all the beautiful things of nature, and the wild creatures are my friends." But it was no longer enough to feel the beauty

Mary Scott Skinker

of nature; now she was engaged in decoding the mysteries of the natural world.

Rachel was fascinated by the cause. She stayed after class to ask questions and continued her talks with Skinker outside the classroom. The brilliant Skinker surely was for Rachel the model of a woman intellectual. They must have made an interesting pair, Rachel, as unfashionable as anyone on campus, and the tall, slender professor who wore stylish dresses. Skinker was, however, more than fashionable. She was academically rigorous. She respected effort and abhorred laziness. One student, an art major, had worked hard on her lab notebooks, which were both accurate and well-drawn. Skinker gave her high grades on them, even though the young woman was not a particularly good science student.

On the other hand, obvious sloth was rewarded with the grade it deserved. Skinker gave the most popular girl in Rachel's class a C. When the student's wealthy parents protested, President Coolidge pressured Skinker to change the grade. Skinker refused, only adding to her campus mystique.

Rachel, fascinated by this new world of biology, thought at first she could no longer write. On a paper for English professor Croff, she wrote, "I have gone dead! And have been since semesters." By the end of that second year, however, she had produced a number of fine essays and stories. One was a quirky piece that began, "You think I am a Pessimist? Who wouldn't be if they were in my place? . . . No one in this household pays any attention to me." The speaker was a cat in a household that cared little for cats.

One winter night, Rachel sat reading Croff's English

assignment, Alfred, Lord Tennyson's poem "Locksley Hall." In the poem, a young man ruminates about his lost love as he waits to board ship. The poem closes with the lines,

> Comes a vapour from the margin, blackening
>   over heath and holt,
> Cramming all the blast before it, in its breast a
>   thunderbolt.
>
> Let it fall on Locksley Hall, with rain or hail, or
>   fire or snow;
> For the mighty wind arises, roaring seaward, and
>   I go.

The last line remained with Rachel all her life. Years later she wrote to a friend, "On a night when rain and wind beat against the windows of my college dormitory room, a line from 'Locksley Hall' burned itself into my mind," and she quoted the words accurately. "I can still remember my intense emotional response," she said, "as that line spoke to something within me seeming to tell me that my own path led to the sea—which then I had never seen—and that my own destiny was somehow linked with the sea."

Rachel was torn. She thought about changing her field to biology, but after talks with both Croff and Skinker, she decided to remain an English major with a minor in science. And she hadn't "gone dead." Her short story "Broken Lamps" won the prestigious Omega literary prize and was published in *The Englicode* on her twentieth birthday. The main character is a engineer who wants to design a bridge that is the perfect combination of beauty and function—representing the tension between art and science, perhaps? And that tension is mirrored in the engineer's marital difficulties, another subject familiar to Rachel.

Summer in Springdale was a reminder of Rachel's other world. Her sister Marian had left her second husband and was living in the Carson house with her two young children. By August, Robert Jr.'s troubled marriage was over, and he, too, lived at home. Rachel, one imagines, looked forward to fall and the start of school.

THREE

An Adventurous Mind

RACHEL BEGAN HER junior year enrolled in both English and science classes. It was a busy time. She played goalie on the hockey team, wrote for the school papers, and for the first time had several good friends. Mary Frye and Dorothy Thompson, both a year behind her, were as excited by Skinker's science classes as Rachel. Marjorie Stevenson, a history major, became her closest friend. She, too, had read the classics, and, like Rachel, she had an independent streak and a sense of humor. Both believed college should teach you to think, not simply force you to memorize facts. Education, they argued, should be a great adventure of the mind.

Skinker's classes were indeed an adventure, increasing Rachel's delight in the world of biology. Even as she wondered again about changing her major, her writing became more elegant. For an English class exercise studying different poetic forms, she wrote:

Butterfly poised on a thistle's down,
Lend me your wings for a summer's day.
What care I for a kingly crown,
Butterfly poised on a thistle's down,
When I might wear your gossamer gown,
And sit enthroned on an orchid spray?
Butterfly poised on a thistle's down,
Lend me your wings for a summer's day!

The form is called a triolet, a poem in eight lines with a rhyming pattern of abaaabab. The first, fourth, and seventh lines are the same, as are the second and eighth. It is an intellectual challenge to fit your words to that complex pattern and at the same time have a transcendent theme. Students in the class had vivid memories of the scene:

We settled back to hear Miss Croff read the best of our creations. Most of them were really plodding. Then came this one. . . . The whole class fairly fell at her feet. "How did you do it?" we asked. "Well," she said, "I knew a triolet was supposed to be light, so I thought of the lightest things I could, a butterfly and thistle down." She was a little embarrassed, possibly, for the rest of us who had been so inept.

That fall was Rachel's best on the hockey field. To play on the team, a student had to maintain good grades and regularly attend practices. Although initially a substitute, Rachel clocked more playing time than many others. When the team's goalie flunked Latin, Rachel, dressed in the standard "baggy blue bloomers, black silk stockings, and high white tennis shoes," took over the position. "She turned out to be a whiz," said a classmate. "She had a hard-hitting accuracy, and a certain concentration that seldom let a puck past her."

Field hockey was so popular, students organized two honorary teams, Army and Navy. Rachel was Navy's goalie. She volunteered to find a goat, the traditional Navy mascot. On the day of the game, she arrived with two. *The Arrow* printed the list of team members: "Extras—Two goats (one vicious, the other too young

PCW hockey team, Rachel in back row, second from right.

to know better), and some dogs." In the last quarter of the game, a dog raced onto the field and bit the ball. The ensuing rumpus angered the older goat, who then charged onto the field, causing havoc. The final score: Navy 7, Army 2, dog and goat tethered.

By winter, Rachel again considered changing her major to biology. Had she worried about getting a job after graduation, the decision would have been easy. Writing was a respectable profession for women, a safe choice. On the other hand, there were few women scientists. Most worked either as teachers or as fairly low-level government researchers.

But Rachel loved biology. Although "reserved" as her friend Dorothy had said, Rachel wasn't afraid of risks. She made the change; somehow she'd find work in this field she loved. Not everyone approved. Miss Coolidge, in her role as college president, thought that as a writer, Rachel could be a success; as a scientist, she wasn't sure. Some students also disapproved. "I've gotten bawled out and called all sorts of blankety-blank names so much that it's beginning to get monotonous. That's all from the other girls, of course." One class-mate told Rachel, "Anyone who can write as well as you can is NUTS to switch to biology!"

That winter was a happy one for Rachel. After a major snowfall, a group of students took trays from the dining hall and spent an evening sledding on the hillside by the amphitheater. In an article for *The Arrow*, Rachel wrote, "I sing of trays . . ." Later, dried and in pajamas, the sledders ate sandwiches and drank coffee before a fire in the dorm living room. "That was one of the nicest times I've had since I came to college," Rachel told Mary. "I wouldn't have missed it for anything."

Rachel had only a year and a half left to fulfill the requirements for graduating with a major in biology. She dropped some English classes and added science courses. She was interested in zoology, the study of animals, with particular emphasis on marine life. She also continued to write for the school publications and play sports. And she scrambled to get ready for the junior prom. Her silver slippers were tight, and so she wore them days in advance to stretch them out. It must have worked, since she had "a glorious time." Rachel's date was a junior at Westminster College, and they went out several more times. But Rachel, it seems, spent most of her time taking the courses she needed to graduate in her new field.

Spring brought a shocker—Mary Scott Skinker would be on a leave of absence during Rachel's senior year. Tensions between Skinker and Coolidge had escalated, with Skinker encouraging students like Rachel to take science studies seriously and Coolidge downplaying the importance of science training for young women, who were, after all, destined to be homemakers.

There was another problem. Coolidge had said department heads had to have a Ph.D. in their field, and Skinker had only a masters degree. She decided to complete course work for her doctorate at Johns Hopkins. In April, Rachel thought she'd follow Skinker. Johns Hopkins admitted some students without a bachelors degree into its graduate programs if their academic records merited it. Telling only her friends Mary Frye and Marjorie Stevenson, Rachel applied for early admission, and a month later was accepted. But students without a B.A. had to pay a higher tuition. Rachel, already in debt to PCW, needed a full scholarship. As she waited to hear from Hopkins, she wrote Mary, "In lots of ways I'd hate not to graduate with my class. I wish I wasn't always having to make these awful decisions." The decision was made for her. Johns Hopkins didn't offer her enough money.

With her junior year of dramatic change at last over, Rachel went home to Springdale. Unusually for the Carson household, it was a relatively peaceful summer. Rachel worked on a biology project she'd brought home and earned money tutoring two high-school students in Latin, English, and geometry.

That summer Mary Skinker had a coveted research position at the Marine Biology Laboratory (MBL) at Woods Hole on Cape Cod. Every summer scientists from around the world arrived at MBL to carry on research projects. "To be engrossed in one's work is good form here," Skinker wrote Rachel, "and that's what I enjoy most." She also enclosed information about MBL. Thrilled, Rachel told Mary Frye that they should try to go the following year. "It must be a biologist's paradise."

Over the summer Rachel and Mary Frye planned to form a PCW science club named Mu Sigma, the Greek letters for Skinker's initials. Rachel expected trouble from Coolidge. The administration, she wrote Mary, "would just as leave there weren't any science majors." When school began, however, the two were surprised to find that Coolidge approved the plan. The academic year, however, brought another sadness. Grace Croff, Rachel's English professor and first college mentor, did not return to PCW. Rachel assumed, as she did about Skinker, that the college was at fault.

Skinker's replacement was Dr. Anna R. Whiting. She was the first married woman faculty member at

PCW. Whiting had a doctorate from a state agricultural university in eugenics, the study of improving species through selective reproduction. She had worked in cattle-breeding programs. Both her training and interests were very different from Skinker's. Laboratory work was not her forte, nor was she interested in field trip research. She did teach courses in histology, embryology, and genetics.

To make up for lost time, Rachel packed into this last year the new science classes, plus physics, and organic chemistry. That alone would have been an astonishing course load; she also studied German. Both Rachel and Dorothy reported to Skinker that Whiting's classes were "a farce" and she was singularly inept in the laboratory. They worried that they wouldn't be able to manage graduate work with such slipshod training. Although Skinker had agreed to Whiting's appointment, she apologized. "You can never realize how sorry I am the way things have gone this year."

By the end of Rachel's senior year, she owed PCW $1,600. The debt had to be cleared in order for her to graduate. The Carsons, rich in land and poor in cash, deeded to Rachel two Springdale lots, which she then transferred to PCW as security against the debt, which she planned to repay.

In the spring, Rachel reapplied to Johns Hopkins and was promptly admitted as a graduate student in the zoology department. On a joyous April day, she received notice that the school had awarded her a full tuition scholarship for her first year. *The Arrow* proclaimed the news:

Rachel Carson '29 Wins Scholarship. . . . The scholarship awarded by Johns Hopkins University is one of seven offered to applicants of high scholastic standing who have given evidence of their ability to carry on independent research. The honor of this award is seldom conferred upon women.

Spring brought more wonderful news. PCW planned to sponsor a graduating student for a summer seat at Woods Hole Marine Biological Laboratory and pay all the registration and lab fees. Before her departure, Skinker had recommended Rachel, and the faculty had agreed. Rachel would spend weeks studying with leading scientists and university professors. Mary Frye, still in college, would pay her own fees and attend as a student. Their dream from the previous summer was about to come true.

Graduation was held on the tenth of June in the college chapel. Rachel was among three in the class of seventy who was awarded her degree magna cum laude. Her parents must have been beaming that Monday afternoon. She was the first in the family to have completed a four-year college program and was headed for advanced studies at a prestigious university.

Their brilliant and talented daughter, however, was delighted to be leaving PCW. "I didn't care a rap myself about receiving the empty honors of PCW," she wrote to Dorothy Thompson the following year, when Dorothy also graduated magna cum laude, "but I knew those who were interested in me would have been disappointed if I hadn't gotten whatever glory was being handed out, and for that reason I was glad."

The yearbook inscription next to Rachel's picture read,

A muse of fire that ascends
The brightest heavens of invention.

Rachel was leaving PCW believing she was now a scientist, no longer a writer. But Marjorie Stevenson wrote in Rachel's yearbook: "Rachel, I want you to remember what I told you about a wild lady biologist. Remember I prophesy you'll be a famous author yet." She added, "Please don't take all the frogs and skeletons too seriously. . . ."

Rachel's college graduation photo, 1929.

FOUR

Roaring Seaward, and I Go

SPRINGDALE HAD BECOME even more polluted since Rachel's childhood. Power plants spewed increasing amounts of toxic waste into both air and water. River traffic had increased, and runoff from factories, combined with oil spills and coal dust, had left the river brown and murky. Still, it was home, and Rachel spent days roaming the woods and fields behind the house. So much in her mother's world had shaped her, but now she was impatient to leave. The ocean she had long dreamed of beckoned.

Rachel left Springdale on a train to Baltimore to look for housing for the fall semester at Johns Hopkins. There was just one dormitory, and it was only for men. She found a room off campus, and set out to spend a few days with Mary Skinker, who was staying at a family mountain cabin in Skyland, Virginia.

Rachel arrived at the foot of the mountain and rode

horseback the four miles to the Skinker cabin. The two women, by now good friends, spent several days playing tennis, hiking in the hills, horseback riding, and, most pleasurable of all, talking. Mary Skinker was Rachel's guide to the world of science, where few women had traveled. The roadblocks and difficult choices she had made were all ones Rachel would face.

At PCW, when Skinker had appeared for dinner with a flower pinned to her shoulder or waist, students had guessed there was a secret admirer. How right they were, but Skinker had broken off her engagement. She didn't believe she could have a career and a marriage as well. It wasn't an easy choice in those days. A married woman was expected to stay home with her family, and a single woman was viewed as "unnatural," since she wasn't a wife and mother. Rachel had no illusions about marriage. Her sister was twice divorced; her brother, once. Rachel yearned to explore the world of biology, and like Skinker, she believed she had to be single-minded in pursuit of her goal.

After several lovely days, Rachel and Mary Skinker took a last long walk down the mountain. Early the next morning Rachel traveled to Massachusetts. "The

[boat] trip over to Woods Hole was glorious in the early morning, which was clear and cold." One can only imagine the dizzying excitement, the irrepressible smile as she gripped the ship's railing. Rachel Carson, having dreamed of the ocean since early childhood, was at last "at sea."

It isn't often that reality is as splendid as one's dreams, but Woods Hole was—its research laboratories with a long expanse of windows facing the ocean, species and habitats to explore, and a collegial world encouraging talk. The research library was filled with books and publications from the around the world. Rachel later said here was the genesis of her best seller *The Sea Around Us*, when she "began storing away facts about the sea." It was a place where commitment to one's work was not just respected but expected.

Rachel stayed at Woods Hole for six weeks. Her expenses were minimal. She and Mary Frye shared a room for four dollars a week and ate at the MBL dining room for seven dollars a week. Rachel's "tuition" was paid for by PCW. It was, as Rachel had thought, a "biologist's paradise." Researchers sat at lab tables with others working on related projects. Dining was family style, and conversation was always lively. Women were fully integrated—there were no separate women's laboratory areas or tables.

"One can't walk very far in any direction," Rachel wrote Dorothy, "without running into water." For the first time, Rachel saw marine creatures in their own environment, not in test tubes or drawings. How do scallops swim, she might have wondered. Rachel watched as they opened their shell halves. Then, as if taking a bite out of the water, they clapped them shut, sending out a stream that propelled them forward, back, up, down, or sideways. And what did they see out of those thirty to forty blue eyes that lined their shell edges?

Summer at Woods Hole was not just about the life of the mind. Mary taught Rachel to swim, they played tennis, and they sat on the beach "adding to our sunburn. . . . I've completely despaired of ever getting *brown*," Rachel wrote Dorothy. "However I am getting sort of weathered-looking, besides growing a crop of freckles." There were picnics and cheerful, noisy social gatherings at night. Rachel was the most carefree she'd ever been, with no worries about family.

Dr. R. P. Cowles, a marine biologist from Johns Hopkins, was also at Woods Hole that summer. He would be one of Rachel's professors come the fall, and they talked about her research project for her master's degree. "Nothing," she wrote Dorothy, "has ever been done on the terminal nerve in any reptiles except the turtle, so I've decided to work on it in lizards and snakes, and maybe crocodiles." Rachel learned just how inadequate Dr. Whiting's classes had been. "You may be glad you aren't taking any more courses from A.R.W.," she wrote. "The less you can have to do with biology at P.C.W. the better."

Rachel on Woods Hole research boat, 1929.

Rachel read, worked in the lab, walked the shoreline, laughed with friends, and knew with absolute certainty she'd found her world.

Before school started, Rachel visited Elmer Higgins, acting Director of the U.S. Bureau of Fisheries. What job opportunities were there, Rachel wanted to know, for women in science, and in particular marine biology? What was the work of the Fisheries Bureau? Higgins was forthright. The biological sciences encompassed the whole world of nature and offered all sorts of research positions . . . for men. Not for women. Neither Higgins nor Rachel knew that a catastrophic stock market crash was only weeks away, and that the Great Depression would be as limiting a factor in Rachel's search for work as her gender.

Rachel's university class load included organic chemistry, a famously difficult course where she was one of two women in a class of about seventy men. When she scored an 85 on the exam, she wrote Mary Frye, "I was never so proud of an 85 in my life!"

Rachel had studied comparative anatomy with Skinker at PCW. When Professor Cowles reviewed her college notebooks, he decided her work was good enough for her to skip the class. But in her genetics course with Professor H. S. Jennings, a world-famous biologist, she realized again how weak Anna Whiting's course had been. Her physiology class was taught by Dr. Mast, known as "the terror of all [degree] aspirants at Hopkins." Mast did not grade his final exams, but commented on them. On Rachel's paper he'd written "very good." Skinker later told Dorothy Thompson, "*I'd* be walking in the clouds if *I* had such an achievement to my credit. [Rachel] need do nothing more and yet she would remain the envy of many there."

Rachel was happy at Johns Hopkins. "The professors are splendid to work with," she told Mary, "and the students are a dandy crowd." But "the lab," she wrote Dorothy, "is my world and is going to be my chief existence until I get my degree."

Rachel would soon again be surrounded by family. Her father was in poor health, certainly not helped by the stress of the Depression. In 1929, when the stock market collapsed, businesses across the country, and indeed throughout the world, shut down. Some 16 million Americans lost their jobs. Rachel's family decided they could live more cheaply in one household than separately.

Rachel rented a house outside of Baltimore, and her parents joined her in the spring of 1930. Job prospects were better in Baltimore than in Pittsburgh, and her parents helped as much as they could from their meager funds. Marian and her daughters came later in June. The house was larger than the Springdale farm and had the distinct advantage of indoor plumbing. Rachel was delighted by the "lovely woods at the very back door, a tennis court, a grove of oak trees," and a "big open fireplace." The first semester at Johns Hopkins had been the longest time Rachel and her mother had ever been apart. From this moment until her mother's death, Maria Carson was always a member of Rachel's household. Her mother assumed housekeeping duties, and Rachel, never thrilled with life in the kitchen, was grateful.

Rachel's friend Dorothy Thompson visited the Carson family in their new home. Although other PCW students hadn't liked Mrs. Carson, Dorothy found her to be a "kind woman. . . . She supported Rachel in every way. We got along because I understood that Rachel was her life." Rachel was mindful of her mother's sacrifices and grateful for her support. But Mrs. Carson was always present, and there must have been moments when Rachel would have liked more time alone or with her friends.

As the Depression deepened, more businesses folded, and still more people were out of work. In this economically collapsing world, Rachel had a family to support. She had to find a job.

Grace Lippy, who taught an undergraduate zoology course for Johns Hopkins during the summer, hired Rachel as a laboratory assistant. Rachel was responsible for washing and laying out equipment for forty-five students, and helping them with their experiments. Lippy thought Rachel wonderfully calm and patient with the students. The two worked so well together, they continued the partnership for the next four summer sessions.

Rachel was awarded the same scholarship amount for her second year, but tuition had risen. Her summer salary paid for the family expenses, with a small portion going toward reducing the PCW debt. There was nothing left to pay the increased tuition. Rachel had to turn down the scholarship. She became a part-time student and searched for work during the school year. She found a job as a lab assistant at the Johns

Hopkins Institute for Biological Research. In addition, she carried a heavy school load, leaving little time for her own research. "It's a pretty up-hill business to do even the work for the courses," she wrote Dorothy. "It's worse this year than ever before. I feel sometimes as though I'm not getting anywhere as far as the degree is concerned." Her frustration was tinged with some bitterness: "This business of doing two things at once doesn't work . . . unless you're an Amazon."

Rachel struggled to complete her master's thesis. Her work on reptiles had not produced usable results, and so she gave that up for study of a particular squirrel. That, too, fell through, for "the squirrels would not breed. . . . No embryos, no problem, was the situation in a nutshell."

Rachel always worried about money. In February, she wrote the PCW financial office that she couldn't make the monthly payments on her college debt. This was, she wrote, "of considerable worry to me." The letter, all the more poignant for its restraint, shows the enormous strain she functioned under:

To tell of the difficulties which the widespread

depression and unemployment have brought to our household would be only to repeat the story which you are hearing on all sides, I am sure. However, the combination of circumstances has been a little more than I could cope with. We have had prolonged illness in the family since last summer, with all the attendant increase in expenses and elimination of practically all income except my own. As a result, we have been so heavily dependent upon my earnings for the bare necessities of living that there was just *nothing* to send you last month, and I am sorry to say that for the next month or so at least I can see no better prospects.

Brother Robert had joined the family in Baltimore in early 1931. Although he found work in a radio repair shop, in the depths of the Depression, workers were sometimes paid in unusual ways. On one job he received three-fifths of the bill in cash, with the balance in "Mitzi," a Persian cat, and her kittens. Although Rachel had grown up with lots of cats on the farm, her favorite childhood animal pals had been dogs. Mitzi and her brood changed that. Over the years, Buzzie, Kito, Tippy, Muffin, Moppet, and Jeffie all joined Rachel's family.

Rachel continued her summer work with Grace Lippy. "I learned something of the delight," she wrote Dorothy, "that comes from working with alert minds with a real capacity for thought and originality." During the school year, she worked as a biology instructor at the Dental and Pharmacy School of the University of Maryland. She was the only female biology instructor on that staff.

The new job meant money, but caused further delays in work on her thesis. And Rachel needed a new topic. Catfish embryos seemed promising. Rachel planned a study of the so-called "head kidney" in catfish. This organ forms shortly after the fish egg is fertilized and functions like a kidney until the adult kidney develops and takes over.

Rachel read books and articles in English, German, Italian, and French. She dissected hundreds of embryos, prepared slides for microscopic examination, and made drawings from the slides. But with classes, lab work, and the seventy-mile round-trip commute between Johns

Hopkins in Baltimore and the University of Maryland in College Park, Rachel fell behind and was unable to graduate on schedule.

She completed her thesis in the spring of 1932 and passed her oral examination in May. She had produced an "excellent review of the literature on the subject," according to the thesis review committee, and had examined the material from an "exceptionally critical point of view." At last on June 14, 1932, Rachel was awarded her master's degree.

Rachel had planned to continue at Johns Hopkins in the fall, working toward her Ph.D. degree. She enrolled in an advanced zoology course and continued to teach in Maryland. But with the deepening economic depression, the situation of the Carson family, like that of so many other Americans, worsened. Rachel's sister and brother worked only sporadically—Marian was often sick, and Robert had trouble finding steady employment. And her father's health deteriorated. In the fall of 1933, Rachel, often the only one earning any income, was forced to drop out of the Ph.D. program.

Life experiences, however, are rarely wasted. Rachel had been doing research on eels when she left Johns

Hopkins. By altering the salt level in water, she had tried to mirror the changing salinity conditions during eel migrations from river to sea. Ten years later, in her first book about the ocean world, *Under the Sea-Wind*, one of the lead "characters" was an eel, whose life she would describe in vivid, riveting detail.

Rachel's money problems continued. "Deep and sincere as my regret has been that I have been unable to send you regular payments," she wrote PCW, "I nevertheless feel that my first duty is to my parents, and it is literally true that every dollar of my salary is needed to provide bare necessities." She turned over to the college the property the Carsons had put up as collateral, ending her debt.

Rachel looked for a full-time teaching position, but such jobs were scarce. For nearly two years, the only work she could find was with Grace Lippy in the Johns Hopkins summer school program. Desperate to earn more money, Rachel revised poems and short stories she had written in college and submitted them to several magazines, including *Reader's Digest* and the *Saturday Evening Post*. Nobody wanted any of her work. But pen in hand, reworking words and phrases, she found her love of writing rekindled despite the rejection letters.

Then on July 6, 1935, Rachel's family circle was abruptly altered. Her father came into the kitchen saying he felt ill. Maria Carson watched as her husband went out the back door, then pitched forward onto the grass. She reached him moments before he died. Mrs. Carson shipped her husband's body back to Pennsylvania where his sisters lived, but no one from Rachel's immediate family attended the funeral. There was no money for the trip.

FIVE

Seven-Minute Fish Tales

RACHEL NEEDED A JOB. In 1935 she took the federal civil service exams in zoology at Mary Skinker's suggestion. Skinker also encouraged Rachel to talk again with Elmer Higgins, now the division chief of the Bureau of Fisheries, which gathered all kinds of research material about marine life and the fishing industries it supported. Higgins had no job openings, but he did have a problem. His staff was expected to produce fifty-two radio scripts for educational broadcasts. His scientists knew their biology, but their writing was technical and dull. The series, officially titled "Romance Under the Waters," was referred to by the staff as the "seven-minute fish tales."

Could she write? Higgins asked. Rachel explained she'd started in college as an English major and had

Rachel with Rags at her Maryland home.

written articles and stories for the college literary publications. "I've never seen a written word of yours," he said, "but I'm going to take a sporting chance." He offered her a trial run at writing several scripts. Rachel passed with flying colors. Delighted to have found a biologist who could write, Higgins hired her as a part-time employee with a salary of thirteen dollars a week. "I had given up writing forever," Rachel said. "It never occurred to me [when switching majors] that I was merely getting something to write about."

And write she did. Rachel expanded material from the radio scripts into full-length articles for the *Baltimore Sun*. The Sunday magazine editor looked forward to her submissions. "I am glad to hear from you again," he wrote, "particularly to know that you are going on with the writing which you do so well."

Rachel's first piece for the *Sun*, on the shad fishing industry, had introduced her readers to the idea that loving shad roe, a kind of fish egg, was not enough. If you didn't pay attention to the fish as well as the eggs, you risked losing both. The shad population decline, she wrote, was largely the result of destructive fishing methods and pollution. Rachel sounded an alarm: "If this favorite of the Chesapeake Bay region is to hold its own against the forces of destruction, regulations must be imposed which consider the welfare of the fish as well as that of the fisherman."

The article byline was R. L. Carson. Throughout her years of government service, Rachel used her initials rather than her full name. This was by decision, not accident. Since her articles for government publications dealt "largely with economic questions, the scientific basis of conservation measures, etc., we [Rachel and her supervisors] have felt that they would be more effective . . . if they were presumably written by a man." It was, of course, to Higgins's credit that he recognized the valuable resource he had in Rachel. But it was also a reflection of the ingrained sexism of society as a whole that such a deception was considered necessary.

The *Sun* paid Rachel twenty dollars for the article, the equivalent of almost two weeks' pay. A month later Higgins asked Rachel to write an introduction to a brochure about the sea. Rachel handed in her essay, "The World of Waters," and waited as Higgins sat at his desk turning the pages. "My chief read it and handed it back with a twinkle in his eye. 'I don't think it will do,' he said.

'Better try again. But send this one to the *Atlantic*.'"

Rachel must have felt startled and gratified at his response. The *Atlantic Monthly* was one of the leading literary magazines. But perhaps she thought the *Atlantic* was reaching too high, for she put the "literary" version in a desk drawer and revised the piece for bureau use. When Rachel learned the *Reader's Digest* was sponsoring a contest for new writers with a prize of one thousand dollars, she revised the piece and sent it off, but never heard from them. Back in the drawer it went for another year.

In the 1930s and until 1972, the U.S. Civil Service Commission listed female and male job applicants separately. Rachel placed highest on the women's roster for a new full-time junior aquatic biologist position. Higgins wanted her, and in August she was officially appointed to the Bureau of Fisheries at a salary of two thousand dollars a year, a reasonable amount, although barely enough to support her family. She was one of only two women who worked for the bureau not in a secretarial position.

In her new job, Rachel analyzed data on Chesapeake Bay marine life, wrote and edited scientific reports, and prepared material for the public. She continued to send ideas to the *Baltimore Sun*, and wrote seven articles in the first six months of the year. Rachel took field trips to sites, visited commercial facilities, interviewed fishermen and factory owners, read the scientific literature, and consulted with other scientists to clarify and check material. Over the sixteen years Rachel worked in government, she established a network of colleagues with whom she remained in contact when she became a full-time writer.

Rachel always had a notebook with her in which she recorded facts, impressions, sensory information about all manner of things. She noticed who scrambled for cover when the tide went out, how a bird's song changed at different times, who nibbled on what part of a flower, how the sounds of rain differed on the beach and in the forest. Listening, seeing, smelling, feeling, she let her senses take in the world around her.

The year 1937 began with another family tragedy. Rachel's sister Marian, who had been ill for a long time, died of pneumonia. She left two young daughters, ages twelve and eleven, in Rachel and Mrs. Carson's care. To reduce expenses and shorten travel time, Rachel looked for a new home closer to her office. She rented a house in Silver Spring, Maryland, and she, her mother, and her two nieces, plus the cats, moved at the beginning of July. Although not yet thirty years old, Rachel was now the family's sole breadwinner. She pulled out "The World of Waters" essay, revised it yet again, and sent it off to the *Atlantic Monthly*, a year after Elmer Higgins had made that suggestion.

The response was swift. Edward Weeks, acting editor, wrote, "We have everyone of us been impressed by your uncommonly eloquent little essay. . . . The findings of science you have illuminated in such a way as to fire the imagination of the layman." Weeks made two suggestions: cut the lead paragraph and shorten the title to "Undersea." Rachel instantly agreed. Like many writers, she thought she could always improve her work. In typical fashion she revised much more than the opening paragraph. She might never have declared it finished had there not been an immutable deadline.

The *Atlantic* published "Undersea" by R. L. Carson in its September 1937 issue. Rachel explained to Weeks the reason behind the use of her initials. She did, however, put one foot out the door: she agreed to allow her full name in the column describing the issue's contributors.

Lyrical and evocative, Rachel's essay instantly engaged the reader:

Who has known the ocean? Neither you nor I, with our earth-bound senses, know the foam and surge of the tide that beats over the crab hiding under the seaweed of his tide-pool home; or the lilt of the long, slow swells of mid-ocean, where shoals of wandering fish prey and are preyed upon, and the dolphin breaks the waves to breathe the upper atmosphere.

Rachel took the reader on a tour from the shoreline to the edge of the continental shelf and then down to the ocean floor. Back at the shore's edge, the reader watched with her:

At last comes a tentative ripple, then another, and finally the full, surging sweep of the incoming tide. The folk of the pools awake—clams stir in the mud. Barnacles open their shells and begin a rhythmic sifting of the waters. One by one, brilliant-hued flowers blossom in the shallow water as tube worms extend cautious tentacles.

Perhaps the most telling phrase is "the folk." Rachel was not attributing human characteristics to other species. Rather, she understood that marine animals, like people, search for food, hide from enemies, make homes.

It was Rachel's achievement in her writings to create images that reflect complex biological reality, yet can be understood by the average reader:

Every living thing of the ocean, plant and animal alike, returns to the water at the end of its own life span the materials that had been temporarily assembled to form its body. So there descends into the depths a gentle, never-ending rain of the disintegrating particles of what once were living creatures of the sunlit surface waters.

As she herself recognized, "From those four *Atlantic*

pages . . . everything else followed." It began when Quincy Howe, senior editor at Simon & Schuster publishers, wrote her to say he'd "enjoyed the undersea article" and asked if she "was planning a book on the same general subject." It was an intriguing thought. "I had never seriously considered writing a book, but naturally that letter put ideas in my head."

Hendrik van Loon, noted journalist and historian, also wrote to Rachel describing his delight at her piece. "Maybe Jules Verne and his 20,000 leagues under the sea started me sixty years ago but I have always wanted to read something about that mysterious world and suddenly . . . in the *Atlantic*, most appropriately . . . I found your article which shows that you are the woman . . . [who can help me]." Howe was van Loon's editor, and five months later, Rachel met with the two to discuss the idea of a book about the sea. Before Simon & Schuster would give her a contract, however, she had to show them several chapters.

Rachel loved the research and combined work with vacation. In 1938, she, her mother, and her two nieces took a ten-day trip to a beach near Beaufort, North Carolina. "Most people stay within sight of the piers and boardwalks of a resort beach," she wrote. "I always seek out the wild sections of beach." She spent hours walking the dunes, lying on the sand "saturating myself with the sounds of water and the feel of hot sun and blowing sand."

Some of Rachel's experiences on that North Carolina beach appeared three years later in her book *Under the Sea-Wind*. Every fall, for one example, many young fish, including mullet, leave ponds and estuaries and travel far out into the sea to spawn. "The first chill of fall stirred in the fish the feeling of the sea's rhythm and awakened the instinct of migration." The young fish were freed for their long trip: "Leaping and racing, foaming and swirling, the incoming flood brought release to the myriads of small fishes that had been imprisoned in the pond. Now in thousands they poured out of the pond and out of the marshes. They raced in mad confusion to meet the clean, cold water."

Years later Rachel told a friend of her intensely emotional response as she watched this small moment of a life cycle that had been repeated from time immemorial. "Of course . . . I didn't tell it as a personal experience, but it was—I stood knee-deep in that racing water and at times could scarcely see those darting, silver bits of life for my tears."

Rachel continued to write articles, for as the sole support of her mother and two young nieces, she was barely making ends meet. In a year and a half she wrote a piece virtually every month. She continued to touch on the themes she had raised in her first *Baltimore Sun* article—wasteful, destructive industry practices and pollution. "For three centuries we have been busy upsetting the balance of nature by draining marshlands, cutting timber, plowing under the grasses that carpeted the prairies. Wildlife is being destroyed. But the home of wildlife is also our home."

Rachel now proposed an idea to the *Sun* about another kind of pollution. She wanted to examine the dangerous effects of selenium and certain fluorides in the soil. "It has been known for a good while," she wrote, "that stock was being poisoned from this source and there is some recent work which indicates that people may not fare so well when their drinking water is polluted in this fashion."

At the same time, she continued to work on the *Sea-*

Wind book. Perhaps from a lifelong pattern of independent thinking, perhaps from a deeply ingrained sense of privacy, or perhaps because she wasn't yet certain of the outcome, Rachel told no one the subject of the book. Her friend and colleague Dorothy Hamilton was at Woods Hole with Rachel in the summer of 1939. Although Dorothy and Rachel shared living quarters and spent a fair amount of time together, Dorothy knew only that Rachel was working on a book, not its content. "I was getting more and more curious," Dorothy said, "but knew nothing more until the book was published. We were very surprised and tremendously excited."

When Rachel returned home from Woods Hole, she began work at the U.S. Fish and Wildlife Service (FWS), the new name for the Bureau of Fisheries. Outside of the office, Rachel worked on the book. She wrote mostly at night and on weekends, and occasionally very early in the morning before going to her office. At last in the early spring of 1940, she submitted five chapters to Simon & Schuster. This was her first attempt at a long piece of writing. Would they want to publish it? The answer came by return mail. Simon &

Schuster sent a book contract and a small check. Rachel, at last, was reaching her "vision splendid."

"From that time on the writing went a lot faster, because a deadline had been set and I was writing under pressure, which sometimes isn't a bad thing."

A manuscript page from *Under the Sea-Wind*,
with sketch of Rachel's cat Buzzie.

SIX

Superb Indifference

RACHEL USUALLY WROTE her first drafts by hand. She'd read aloud to herself to hear the sounds and rhythms of the phrases, and then revise over and over. Years later she wrote E. B. White, "I was delighted to find you saying that you 'write by ear, always with difficulty, and seldom with any exact notion of what is taking place under the hood.' This describes my method, or lack of one, precisely."

Rachel worked alone in a large upstairs bedroom. Actually, not entirely alone. "My constant companions during those otherwise solitary sessions were two precious Persian cats, Buzzie and Kito." Buzzie often slept on top of a "litter of notes and manuscript sheets." Rachel occasionally stopped writing and made sketches of him with "his little head drooping with sleepiness, then of him after he had settled down comfortably for a nap."

Most books about nature are written from the viewpoint of people. Rachel was "determined to avoid this human bias as much as possible." In part one of the book, the main character is a sandpiper known as a sanderling, a bird almost everyone who has ever walked a beach has seen. It was typical of Rachel to choose a common creature, precisely because its uncommon life is so little known. The sanderling makes one of the longest migration trips of any bird, nesting near the North Pole, and wintering as far south as Patagonia at the bottom of South America.

In part two, Rachel began, "as biographies usually do, with the birth of my central character," the mackerel. Of some half a million eggs an adult mackerel may produce in a season, usually only two young survive to adulthood. "This ceaseless ebb and flow of life—the constant destruction of individuals contrasted with the survival of whole species—is one of the most impressive spectacles which the sea presents."

In the final section of the book, Rachel takes us from inland rivers down past the continental shelf to the blackest depths of the sea as we travel with the Anguilla, whose common name is eel. Atlantic eels, both American and European, are born in the Sargasso

Sea in the middle of the Atlantic Ocean. The two species are intermingled at birth and then separate into two great bands of migrants, one headed east, one west. Scientists can distinguish them only "by counting the number of vertebrae in the backbone, but the little eels themselves never make a mistake. They always return to the continent from which their parents came."

To understand the lives of sea creatures, Rachel explained, she had to turn aside human ways of making sense of the world.

Time measured by the clock or the calendar means nothing if you are a shore bird or a fish, but the succession of light and darkness and the ebb and flow of the tides mean the difference between the time to eat and the time to fast, between the time an enemy can find you easily and the time you are relatively safe. We cannot get the full flavor of marine life—cannot project ourselves vicariously into it—unless we make these adjustments in our thinking.

But how do we make sense of another creature's life? Rachel believed:

We must not depart too far from analogy with human conduct if a fish, shrimp, comb jelly, or bird is to seem real to us. . . . For these reasons I have deliberately used certain expressions which would be objected to in formal scientific writing. I have spoken of a fish "fearing" his enemies, for example, not because I suppose a fish experiences fear in the same way that we do, but because I think he *behaves as though he were frightened*. With the fish, the response is primarily physical; with us, primarily psychological. Yet if the behavior of the fish is to be understandable to us, we must describe it in the words that most properly belong to human psychological states.

Humans work to convince themselves they are both unique as a species and superior to others. Rachel reminds us that even with all our differences, we share the planet and have the same fundamental life drives.

In the end, the main character in *Under the Sea-Wind* is the ocean itself. "The smell of the sea's edge," Rachel later wrote, "the feeling of vast movements of water, the sound of waves, crept into every page, and over all was the ocean as the force dominating all its creatures."

After many revisions, Mrs. Carson typed the final version. On the last day of 1940, Rachel sent off the completed manuscript to Simon & Schuster. Shortly before publication and anxious about the book's reception, Rachel wrote to Hendrik van Loon. With the wisdom of a writer who'd been around the block, van Loon wrote back, "It seems to me the older I grow, the more the whole damn business is but a gamble . . . what the public will swallow or not . . . who can tell . . . let us hope this time they prove to be fond of fish."

Rachel had written the book as if she were a reporter "embedded" with the three communities—sanderling, mackerel, and eel—traveling with them as they searched for food, endured fierce weather events, and avoided or succumbed to the jaws of their enemies. For the approach to work, her science had to be accurate and her literary ability stellar. Now she waited for the reviews.

She wasn't disappointed. The *New York Times*, the *New York Herald Tribune*, and the *New Yorker*, among others, praised this new author. The Scientific Book Club Review noted, "There is poetry here, but no false sentimentality. There is ruthlessness as well as beauty in nature." For Rachel, the opinions of scientists were the most important. William Beebe, the famed oceanographer at the New York Zoological Society, reviewed the book favorably for *Saturday Review* and selected two chapters to include in a nature anthology he published several years later.

It was a brief ride in the sun. One month after publication, the Japanese bombed Pearl Harbor, and on December 8, 1941, America plunged into World War II. Although the reviewers had proved "fond of fish," Rachel noted, "the world received the event with superb indifference." Clinging to the hope she would yet make money from book sales, Rachel repeatedly questioned the marketing and publicity people at Simon & Schuster. The reading public, however, was too busy with the war effort to buy books about migrating birds and fish, however beautifully written.

As America mobilized for war, new government agencies sprang into being. Those less directly concerned with wartime efforts were moved out of Washington. In March 1942, Rachel's office was told they'd be relocated to Chicago. She wrote a friend, "I'd rather get into some sort of work that had more immediate value in relation to the war." To feel useful, she took a first-aid class and trained as an air-raid warden.

Mrs. Carson moved with Rachel to Chicago, where Rachel worked on bulletins for a "Food from the Sea" series. War rationing of meat meant people had to rely more on fish for protein. The bulletins were a way to introduce them to little-known seafood. Rachel, however, was unable to write a practical handbook without infusing it with a sense of wonder. In her introduction to the series she wrote, "Our enjoyment of these foods is heightened if we also know something of the creatures from which they are derived, how and where they live, how they are caught, their habits and migrations."

Her brief history of the clam, however, was so engaging, it probably had the unanticipated effect of keeping people from eating them. She took the reader on a journey with the embryonic clam, first as it swam in the surface waters; then three to six days later as it sank to the bottom, anchoring itself with a spun thread to "a bit of seaweed, a stone, or a shell"; and then finally to its burrow on the sea bottom, which "it never again leaves . . . of its own accord."

The move to Chicago was brief, and Rachel was

back in Maryland by the spring of 1943. She was promoted twice with small salary increases, but it was not enough. With little hope for income from *Under the Sea-Wind*, Rachel determined to write magazine articles. After *Reader's Digest* rejected an article about oysters, she wrote a friend, "while it is relatively easy to write about the oddities in nature . . . my real interest is not in the believe it or not type of thing, but in developing a deeper appreciation of nature." Still, she kept trying to sell informational pieces that in the words of the *Digest*'s requirements made "lively reading."

Rachel's article ideas were often based on materials that crossed her desk at FWS. The Japanese occupation of the Pacific islands, for example, meant companies had no access to ceiba trees, the source of kapok stuffing for sleeping bags and life preservers. Botanists suggested using the soft floss of the milkweed plant. Rachel's article, published in 1944 in *This Week* magazine, meant that those strolling along the roadside could view milkweed seedpods overflowing with white, downy tufts as allies in the war effort.

War research had also expanded knowledge of radar. Rachel wrote an article about bats and their sonar-detection skills, similar to radar. "The Bat Knew It First," published in *Collier's*, was later reprinted by the *Reader's Digest*. The U.S. Navy recruiting office called it "one of the clearest expositions of radar yet made available for public consumption," and distributed the piece to recruiting stations.

One of Rachel's articles had as its star the chimney swift, the "fastest small bird in North America":

Not only does it eat in the air, the chimney swift drinks and bathes on the wing, dipping to the surface of a pond for a momentary contact with the water; its courtship is aerial; it sometimes even dies in the sky. . . . It never perches on a tree, never alights on the ground. Its whole existence is divided between the sky and a nocturnal resting place inside a chimney or a hollow tree.

Never one to assert "truth" in the face of uncertainty, Rachel wrote:

Observers have sometimes seen three adult birds tending a nest. The polite but wholly tentative theory is that the parents have engaged a "nurse-maid." More realistic persons scoff at that and say the swift is polygamous. What the truth is, no one actually knows.

Rachel suggested to a friend that unless a book was a best seller, it made more sense to write for magazines—the pieces were shorter and the pay immediate. She also thought about leaving government for a higher-paying job elsewhere. "I'm definitely in the mood to make a change of some sort, preferably to something that will give me more time for my own writing." She contacted the *Reader's Digest*, the New York Zoological Society, and the National Audubon Society. There were no job openings.

SEVEN

Field Mice for Twelve

THE WAR AND post-war years were probably the most social of Rachel's life. She and her FWS colleagues poked fun at "intransigent official ways, small stupidities, and inept pronouncements," according to Shirley Briggs. "Nothing could pass the wry scrutiny of that gathering." Shirley had joined FWS in 1945 as an artist and information specialist. Like many colleagues, she became Rachel's good friend.

One day Rachel's office group learned that an FWS employee in the Chicago office had written a brochure on cooking wild game. The work was "shoddy," with "most of it plagiarized and some of it absurd." Rachel and her colleagues plotted culinary revenge. They prepared a telegram to the Chicago woman alerting her that a writer and photographer from a famous New York magazine were arriving to do a story on a wild game dish, "field mice for twelve." The recipe, they said, was best with mushrooms and white wine.

The group never sent the telegram when they discovered you could go to jail if you used telegraphic services under a false name. But "we had almost as much fun thinking it up, and imagining the scene." Camaraderie spilled over into after-office hours. Rachel and Shirley Briggs, sometimes joined by Carson family friend Alice Mullen, went hiking and birding as often as they could. On a weekend evening, colleagues went to "an astonishing number of parties," with good talk, music, and lots of laughter.

Along with intriguing information about bats, milkweed, and chimney swifts, some disturbing material crossed Rachel's desk. A new pesticide, DDT (dichlorodiphenyltrichloroethane), had been used during the war to kill lice and other disease-bearing insects. After the war, the U.S. Department of Agriculture (USDA) allowed the DuPont corporation to sell it commercially, despite the fact that there were no long-term tests of its toxic effects.

Rachel had edited a press release about DDT studies at the Patuxent Research Refuge in Maryland.

She proposed an article to the *Reader's Digest* on "the whole delicate balance of nature if [the pesticide was] unwisely used," but the *Digest* wasn't interested. The popular press continued to report on the "success" of the new "war" on pests. And Rachel continued to collect information about DDT, but it would be more than a decade before she'd write about it.

By 1946, Rachel was essentially directing Fish and Wildlife's publication program. She had a staff of six, and as she described it, "It is really just the work of a small publishing house." That year Rachel began production of a series of twelve booklets for the public on the national wildlife refuge system. She herself wrote four and coauthored a fifth. Research for the series was in many ways a gift. Rachel packed outdoor gear, traveled with an artist colleague, and spent official work time doing what she loved—observing creatures in their natural habitats, recording impressions, and writing.

The series, titled *Conservation in Action*, was designed to examine "wildlife resources of America . . . the story of the forces that threaten to destroy them, and the efforts we must make . . . to preserve them." Rachel wanted to awaken the public to our history of "reckless waste and appalling destruction" and the fact that "entire species of animals have been exterminated." The loss of forests, grasslands, coastal shores "have afflicted us," she wrote, "with all the evils of soil erosion, floods, destruction of agricultural lands, and loss of wildlife habitats." Above all, the preservation of wildlife habitat is not about "other species," but about preserving as well "man's essential environment."

Several of the booklets explored the refuges for waterfowl from Massachusetts to North Carolina. Rachel planned trips beginning in the spring of 1946 through the fall of 1947. In April, she and Shirley Briggs traveled to Chincoteague, Virginia, to spend time at the waterfowl refuge on Assateague Island. They hiked across streams and along the beach, collected samples, took photographs, and startled the other hotel guests, Shirley recalled. "We presented quite a spectacle on our return to the hotel of an evening . . . when we came lumbering through, wearing old tennis shoes, usually wet, sloppy and be-smudged pants, various layers of jackets, souwesters, and toting all manner of cameras, my magnificent tripod, and Ray's binoculars." Ray, as her FWS friends called Rachel, and Shirley returned

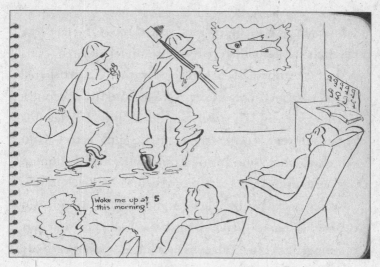

Shirley Briggs's sketches of trip with Rachel
to Chincoteague, Virginia, 1946.

home with sacks of oysters and clams for "culinary research" at a shellfish party Shirley hosted.

In September, Rachel traveled with FWS artist Kay Howe to the Parker River Refuge some thirty miles north of Boston. They were sunburnt, bitten by legions of mosquitoes, and weary from slogging across sand dunes. Rachel, who burned quickly, wore a brimmed hat and draped a scarf from below her eyes down past her neck. Nonetheless, as she wrote a friend, "Of course I'd like to spend all my time doing just that sort of thing, but our budget is not likely to permit very much of it."

Rachel and Kay became quite efficient in their planning. On later trips they brought "an extra-long extension cord for rooms where there was only one electrical outlet, high-wattage light bulbs to read or draw by at night," and perhaps most essential, "a flask of whiskey."

In February Rachel and Kay traveled to Mattamuskeet on the North Carolina coast, a refuge for migrating waterfowl including the endangered whistling swan. In this booklet, Rachel talked about listening. "The name 'whistling swan,'" she wrote, "is given because of a single high note sometimes uttered—a sound that suggests a woodwind instrument in its quality." By comparison the western trumpeter swan "has a deeper, more resonant voice because of an anatomical peculiarity—the windpipe has an extra loop." Mattamuskeet was filled with sounds. When flocks of geese flew overhead, "they would pass over so close," she wrote a friend, "that I could hear the sound of their wings." At the end of 1947, Rachel traveled west to refuges in Utah and Montana and along the Columbia River. On this trip she and Kay got to hear trumpeter swans at the Red Rock Lakes Refuge on the Montana/Idaho border.

The previous summer, Rachel, her mother, and their cats Kito and Tippy had traveled to Maine to spend a month in a rented cottage near Boothbay Harbor. Rachel delighted in the ringing of an ocean buoy, the chatter of sea and forest birds, the rippling of waves, and the brush of wind over sea and land. "The only reason I will ever come back [to D.C.] is that I don't have brains enough to figure out a way to stay here the rest of my life," she wrote Shirley.

Maine beckoned, but the Fish and Wildlife Service paid, and Rachel, as ever, had financial worries. From the mid-1940s on, her work load was heavy. A series of family illnesses added to the stress. Rachel herself was hospitalized three times in two and a half years for relatively minor reasons, her mother had intestinal surgery for a serious problem, and family cat Kito died.

At work, Rachel hired Bob Hines, an artist who became a close friend and collaborator. Hines had at first thought he wouldn't be interested in working for a woman boss, but he liked Rachel and quickly grew to respect her. "She was a very able executive, with almost a man's administrative qualities." She was also special, he said.

She had the sweetest, quietest 'no' any of us had ever heard. But it was like Gibraltar. You didn't move it. She had no patience with dishonesty or shirking in any form and she didn't appreciate anybody being dumb. But she always showed much more tolerance for a dull-minded person who was honest than for a bright one who wasn't. She didn't like shoddy work or shoddy behavior.

To her staff, Rachel was by turns considerate, funny,

insightful, rigorous, calm, and always professional. Her humor, irreverence, and sense of adventure gave Shirley Briggs, whose office was next to Rachel's, "an inaccurate and heady view of government life." Once when Hines brought Rachel sketches, she handed back the drawing of a mullet. "We'd better fix this one, Bob. You've put one spine too many in the dorsal fin." Rachel knew her mullet.

Even with her promotions, Rachel still faced the kind of sex discrimination she'd first heard about more than two decades earlier from Mary Scott Skinker. In 1949, when Rachel's boss was promoted to the head of FWS, she took over his editorial responsibilities, but was not given his grade level or salary.

Rachel's "ideal existence" would be to "live by writing," she told a friend. But she was afraid to give up the salary she and her family desperately needed. "That is my problem right now, and not knowing what to do about it, I do nothing."

That was not entirely true. During this time Rachel was quietly gathering material for a long work about the sea, outlining its history, geography, chemistry, and life forms. Again, few knew exactly what she was doing.

Shirley Briggs joked that Rachel wanted to write a best-selling romance novel, make tons of money, and *then* write about nature. Then Rachel met Marie Rodell, a literary agent.

Rodell, with an outgoing personality, editorial smarts, an extensive knowledge of the publishing world, and a fierce devotion to her clients, was the perfect publishing partner for Rachel.

Not long after they met, Rachel suffered a hard blow. Mary Skinker, age fifty-seven, was dying of cancer. Rachel Carson, she told the hospital staff, was the person to call. Rachel flew to Chicago. On December 19, 1948, Mary Scott Skinker, Rachel's mentor and the person who so totally understood the choices and challenges Rachel would face, died. Never again would Rachel have a friend with whom she shared so similar a life journey.

And so Rachel turned back to the sea for solace.

EIGHT
Can't Stop Researching

BUT BEFORE A new book, there was an old story. Rachel needed money. Marie Rodell pressed her for a sample chapter and an outline she could show publishers. Marie also wanted to sell individual chapters as magazine articles. Both women researched possible prizes and grants. If she received one, Rachel would be able to take a leave of absence from FWS to complete the book.

Rachel began work on a chapter about islands. Her biggest problem, she told Marie, "is that I keep finding so much terribly interesting stuff that I can't stop researching." It's clear why. Islands, she wrote:

> are ephemeral, created today, destroyed tomorrow. With few exceptions, they are the result of the violent, explosive, earth-shaking eruptions of

submarine volcanoes, working perhaps for millions of years to achieve their end. It is one of the paradoxes in the ways of earth and sea that a process seemingly so destructive, so catastrophic in nature, can result in an act of creation.

Rachel reworked her drafts so often there was "not much more left of the original than remained of Krakatoa after the blast."*

After several rejections from magazines, they both agreed Rachel should put all her energy into the book and no longer try to fashion pieces as individual articles. "The next time I suggest one," Rachel wrote, "please drop my letter in the nearest wastebasket."

When Rachel had written about a third of the book, both she and Marie felt it was ready to send out to publishers. Philip Vaudrin, Oxford University Press editor, heard that Rachel was working on a book, and contacted Rodell. When Rachel met Vaudrin, he implied he'd had to pressure Marie to give the book to Oxford. Marie enjoyed Rachel's report of her meeting. "I am no end amused that Vaudrin never saw through that little strategy about your script—apparently in publish-

* See Notes for additional information.

ing as in sex, a man is always more eager for what one seems reluctant to offer him!" Marie then negotiated a contract with Oxford, and Rachel committed to completing the manuscript by March 1950.

If you passed Rachel in the hallway, you might not have noticed her. If you talked with her, you would have registered the clear, intelligent gaze. But you might have done most of the talking, for she was a careful listener, more interested in another's conversation than in hearing her own voice. Yet this quiet, soft-spoken woman had a passionate sense of adventure and a wry sense of humor. Others might think government publications on sailing directions for mariners would be dull as dishwater. For Rachel there were "few better vehicles for arm-chair traveling." She navigated the coast of Norway, explored the shoreline of the Shetlands and Orkneys, then traveled down to sub-arctic islands, all from a booklet called "Coast Pilots and Sailing Directions." Their descriptions of "dangerous reefs and forbidding shores" were as gripping as Conrad's novels of the sea.

One thing troubled Rachel. She herself had no personal knowledge of underwater life. She talked about this with oceanographer William Beebe, and he promised to make all the arrangements so that she'd "be sure of meeting the proper sharks, octopuses, etc." Beebe also wrote a letter to the Saxton Fellowship committee,

Rachel with undersea diving helmet, 1949.

supporting Rachel's application for their award offered to promising writers.

Rachel joined biologists at the Miami Marine Laboratory—at last she herself was going "down under." She strapped on an eighty-four-pound diving helmet, attached weights to her feet, and descended into the deep. She was enchanted. "How exquisitely delicate and varied are the colors displayed by the animals of the reef. . . . I got the feeling of the misty green vistas of a strange, nonhuman world." The weather was gray and stormy, so Rachel was able to make only one brief trip down the ladder. Even so, "the difference between having dived—even under those conditions—and never having dived is so tremendous that it formed one of those milestones of life, after which everything seems a little different."

Rachel had been working full-time while writing at night and on weekends. The strain was great, and at times she would come home too exhausted to work. Then, while she was on the Florida trip, her mother called to say Rachel had won the Saxton Fellowship. The $2,250 award meant she could take a leave to complete the book.

Her next adventure was on surface waters, aboard the FWS research vessel the *Albatross III*. In late July, the ship sailed to the Georges Bank fishing grounds, two hundred miles out in the Atlantic Ocean east of Boston. No woman had ever been aboard the *Albatross*, and long-standing traditions were not easily changed. The idea of one woman with fifty men was unthinkable, and quickly rejected. But government officials must have thought there was safety in numbers, for they reluctantly agreed to Rachel and a friend. Marie Rodell joined Rachel. She joked that she could write an article titled "I Was a Chaperone on a Fishing Boat."

Some of the ship's officers, unhappy that women were aboard, regaled Rachel and Marie with stories of danger and disaster. Hold fast to something, they were warned, for waves sweep across the deck; every voyage results in broken bones; the food is awful, but no matter, violent seasickness would keep the women from eating anyway.

Crashing sounds did awaken the two the first night. "Surely," Rachel thought, "we had been rammed by another vessel. Then a series of the most appalling bangs, clunks, and rumbles began directly over our heads, a rhythmic thundering of machinery that would put any boiler factory to shame." At last they realized these were the ordinary sounds of a fishing vessel. The next morning when the men grinned at the women and asked if they'd slept well, Marie said, "Well, once we thought we heard a mouse, but we were too sleepy to bother."

Albatross nets brought up vast amounts of marine creatures. Some nights Rachel and Marie stayed up to watch the men work. "I think that first glimpse of the net, a shapeless form, ghostly white, gave me a sense of sea depths that I never had before."

In October Rachel took a month's leave of absence from her job to write. She sent chapters for review to experts in different fields. She was a painstaking writer. She revised chapters on tides, waves, currents, marine geology, islands, over and over again. She was determined to use language and evoke images the lay reader could understand. But she wouldn't oversimplify.

By mid-February 1950, she was desperate to be finished. "I feel now," she wrote Marie, "that I'd die if this went on much longer!" It was clear Rachel would never make the March 1 deadline, and so Rodell negotiated an extension until summer. In May Rachel bemoaned that spring was almost over and she'd not taken "a single morning bird walk. . . . I am really upset about it, but don't seem to have the energy to tuck that in, too."

Writing about tides and currents seemed easier than finding a title for the book. Marie and Rachel discarded many—"Return to the Sea," "The Story of the Ocean," "Empire of the Sea," among others. Rachel enlisted her relatives and FWS colleagues in the search. "Out of My Depth," and "Carson at Sea" were their most intriguing contributions. In April Rachel wrote her editor, "We have made so many title suggestions that I'm afraid I have lost track—did we ever mention 'The Sea Around Us'?"

And a title was born, as was a publishing phenomenon. The *New Yorker* magazine's editor, William Shawn, expressed interest in printing one chapter. In the end Shawn decided to publish a condensed version of nine of the fourteen chapters. Although Rachel had become savvy about business negotiations, she was still a relative innocent in the book world. Advance publication in the *New Yorker*, considered by many the premier literary magazine in the country, was advertising one couldn't buy. It would help make *The Sea Around Us* a best seller even before it arrived in stores.

Then the *Yale Review* bought "The Birth of an Island" chapter, and published it in their September issue. "I am still in a daze about all your news," Rachel wrote Rodell, "all I know is how lucky I am to have you."

Maria Carson, now eighty-one, typed the final manuscript, and Rachel sent it off at the beginning of July 1950. Unlike many authors, Rachel knew a great deal about production and said what she thought to her Oxford editor. The book should not look like a standard textbook, she said. The typeface Oxford wanted for the half title page was "bold and starkly severe sans serif," fine for technical material such as FWS published, "but not a book like mine!"

Rachel also had medical concerns. In September she was hospitalized for surgery to remove a breast tumor. She had had a cyst taken out several years earlier in the same breast, and after the new operation Rachel specifically asked if the tumor was malignant. She was told it wasn't. No further treatment was recommended.

The avalanche of accolades began in late 1950, before the book was even published. Rachel won the

Westinghouse Prize of one thousand dollars for excellence in science writing. In February she learned *Sea* might be a Book-of-the-Month Club (BOMC) selection. If that happened, she'd make enough money to quit her job. She dragged Bob Hines into a phone booth down the hall from her office, swore him to secrecy, and whispered the BOMC news.

The following March, Rachel learned she'd been awarded a prestigious Guggenheim Fellowship equal to six months of her FWS salary. Days later Marie Rodell called to say that *Sea* would be a BOMC alternate selection in the summer. Even *Vogue* magazine joined the rush, reprinting a chapter on ocean currents and climate.

On June 2 the *New Yorker* published the first of its three-part series, and Rachel would never again be a private person. She received phone calls, letters by the bag-load, invitations to speak, and she was stunned. "Heavens," she wrote Rodell, "is this all about me—it's really ridiculous!" Rachel was a private person whose public life until that moment consisted of a relatively small circle of family, colleagues, and friends. She literally did not understand the personal attention. "I grow more astounded by events every day. Maybe it is because a book, once it's between covers, seems to have very little to do with me," she wrote Marie. "It's just itself—well, sort of as a child is different from its parents. I'm pleased to have people say nice things about the book, but all this stuff about me seems odd, to say the least."

On a trip with her mother in a town where she knew no one, she assumed she was safe in a beauty parlor. But "the proprietor came over, turned off the drier, and said: 'I hope you don't mind, but there is someone who wants to meet you.' I admit I felt hardly at my best, with a towel around my neck and my hair in pin curls." On that same trip, when Mrs. Carson answered an early morning knock on their motel room door, an autograph-hunting fan rushed in and thrust two books at Rachel, still in bed, clutching the covers.

Six months after publication, Rachel learned she had won the coveted National Book Award for non-fiction. But awards and accolades, while most satisfying, could not alone account for the book's runaway success. There was poetry in the writing, certainly. In her acceptance speech, Rachel said:

The winds, the sea, and the moving tides are what they are. If there is wonder and beauty and majesty in them, science will discover these qualities. If they are not there, science cannot create them. If there is poetry in my book about the sea, it is not because I deliberately put it there, but because no one could write truthfully about the sea and leave out the poetry.

Yet there had to be something more than evocative writing. The fan mail offers a clue. The United States, only six years from the end of World War II, was embroiled in a nuclear arms race and military action in Korea. Many people took comfort in a long view of history. Letters came from a broad spectrum of people. "Most," Rachel explained, "say that it is because the book has taken them away from the stress and strain of human problems . . . that they have welcomed it." People found "release from tension in the contemplation of millions and billions of years—in the long vistas of geologic time in which men had no part—in the realization that, despite our own utter dependence on the earth, this same earth and sea have no need of us."

There were also readers who didn't believe a book

with such a breadth of scientific knowledge could have
been written by a woman. Rachel never called herself
a feminist—she had her hair done regularly at a beauty
parlor, wore a little hat and gloves when called for—but
she certainly had experienced sexism. She ignored it
when she could and wryly pointed it out when given
the opportunity. "Among male readers" of *The Sea
Around Us*, she said,

> there was a certain reluctance to acknowledge
> that a woman could have dealt with a scientific
> subject. Some, who apparently had never read the
> Bible enough to know that Rachel is a woman's
> name, wrote: "I assume from the author's knowl-
> edge that he must be a man." Another addressing
> me properly as *Miss* Rachel Carson, nevertheless
> began his letter "Dear Sir:" He explained his
> salutation by saying that he had always been con-
> vinced that the males possess the supreme intel-
> lectual powers of the world, and he could not
> bring himself to reverse his convictions.

Gender bias was more widespread than a few
letters reflected. Most male reviewers felt compelled to

point out the author was a woman. Jonathan Norton Leonard ended his Sunday *New York Times Book Review*, "It's a pity that the book's publishers did not print on its jacket a photograph of Miss Carson. It would be pleasant to know what a woman looks like who can write about an exacting science with such beauty and precision."* At Oxford, which published the book, an editor who had never before met Rachel said, "You are such a surprise to me. I thought you would be a very large and forbidding woman."

Shirley Briggs knew how to make Rachel laugh. In a drawing she called "Rachel as her readers seem to imagine her," Briggs created a woman of Herculean size, standing in swirling waters, holding a spear in one hand and an octopus in the other. The drawing came in handy. Rachel's mother was interviewing a potential household aide who was clearly unqualified. The woman stared nervously at the picture. "'Oh,' Mrs. Carson explained, 'that's a painting of my daughter Rachel with whom you will have to work closely if you take this position.'" The woman left quickly.

Some reviewers denigrated Rachel's qualifications. After all, she worked in FWS's publications division,

* See Notes for additional information.

UP CLOSE: RACHEL CARSON

not as a research scientist. But perhaps they were more troubled by Rachel's questioning of scientists' elite status. "We live in a scientific age," Rachel said in her National Book Award acceptance speech,

> yet we assume that knowledge of science is the prerogative of only a small number of human beings, isolated and priestlike in their laboratories. This is not true. The materials of science are the materials of life itself. Science is part of the reality of living; it is the what, the how, and the why of everything in our experience.

Some scientists were delighted. Henry Bigelow, oceanographer and Director of the Harvard Museum of Comparative Zoology, wrote her, "the amount of material you have assembled amazes me. Although I have been concerned with the sea for fifty years, you have found a good many facts I hadn't."

Four months after publication, 100,000 copies of *The Sea* had been sold. By Christmas, the public was buying 4,000 books a day. *The Sea* remained on the *New York Times* Best Seller list for eighty-six weeks, accompanied part of the time by a reissued *Under the Sea-Wind*. The *New York Times* reviewer wrote, "The slender, gentle lady who is editor of the United States Fish and Wildlife Service seems to have the best of it. Once or twice in a generation does the world get a physical scientist with literary genius. Miss Carson has written a classic in *The Sea Around Us*. *Under the Sea-Wind* may be another."

With the rush of money, Rachel applied for a leave of absence from her job. Beginning in July, she was free. She started work on a seashore guide for Paul Brooks at Houghton Mifflin publishers. "I am always more interested," she said, "in what I am about to do than in what I have already done."

The idea for Rachel's new book had been conceived in ignorance. A group of friends visiting a Houghton Mifflin editor strolled a Cape Cod beach and performed what they thought was a good deed. Horseshoe crabs littered the sands. The group returned the crabs to the sea, "unaware that this intended act of mercy was interrupting the normal mating procedure." The editor suggested that Houghton Mifflin publish a guide to the seashore to "dispel such ignorance once and for all."

Rachel set off to explore coastlines from Maine to Florida. She knew the book had to be more than the typical guide. How and where creatures made their homes, searched for food, battled for survival—those were the questions that intrigued her.

The shore is an ancient world, for as long as there has been an earth and sea there has been this place of the meeting of land and water. Yet it is a world that keeps alive the sense of continuing creation and of the relentless drive of life. Each time that I enter it, I gain some new awareness of its beauty and its deeper meanings, sensing that intricate fabric of life by which one creature is linked with another, and each with its surroundings.

NINE

She's Done It Again

HER NEW BOOK was not the only thing on Rachel's mind. After vacationing in Maine, she returned home to a family crisis. Her unmarried niece Marjorie was pregnant. An out-of-wedlock pregnancy in the 1950s was devastating. Rachel was fully aware that if the news became public, the scandal would ruin Marjie's life. And as a public figure, Rachel would be affected by the negative publicity as well. Rachel and her mother came up with a story about the father's absence, and then made arrangements for the child's birth.

At the time, Rachel told only Marie Rodell. The extraordinary success of *The Sea Around Us* had to take second place to a family need. Years later she confided in a friend:

> All that followed the publication of *The Sea*—the acclaim, the excitement on the part of the critics

and the public at discovering a "promising" new writer—was simply blotted out for me by the private tragedy that engulfed me at precisely that time. I know it will never happen again, and if ever I am bitter, it is about that.

Rachel's desire to protect her family's privacy came at the moment she herself was no longer a private person. She was inundated with interview and lecture requests. Like many people with a strong sense of privacy, she was also shy. At her first speech before a large audience, she brought a recording of undersea sounds of shrimp, fish, and whales. It would interest the group, she assumed, and use up some of her time.

Numerous colleges and universities wanted to grant her honorary degrees, but she accepted only a handful. "To do even half the things people want, I'd have to be a sort of Alice in Wonderland character, rushing madly in all different directions at once." When she received an honorary doctorate from her own school, Pennsylvania College for Women, she told a former classmate she much preferred walking barefoot in the sand to standing in high heels on a hardwood floor.

When the Drexel Institute of Technology granted

Rachel an honorary doctorate, she spoke to the engineering students about a false distinction between science and literature:

> Scientists are often accused of writing only for other scientists. They are even charged with opposing any attempt to interpret their findings in language the layman can understand. Literature is merely the expression of truth. And scientific truth has power to improve our world only if it is expressed.

Rachel frequently touched on a theme most people associate with her last book, *Silent Spring*, which was not published until 1962. But ten years earlier at a ceremony awarding her the John Burroughs Medal, she warned:

> Mankind has gone very far into an artificial world of his own creation. He has sought to insulate himself, in his cities of steel and concrete, from the realities of earth and water and the growing seed. Intoxicated with a sense of his own power,

he seems to be going farther and farther into more experiments for the destruction of himself and his world.

A few of her readers were worried about other issues. One letter writer accused her of abandoning God in her discussion of evolution. With great restraint, Rachel acknowledged that she accepted the theory of evolution "as the most logical one that has ever been put forward to explain the development of living creatures on this earth." She added she saw no conflict between belief in a creator and science, since evolution can be understood as God's method of creation. In a more pointed, private observation, when her mother commented that the Bible says God created the world, Rachel answered that General Motors had created her Oldsmobile, "but *how* is the question."

For the first time in her life, with the success of *The Sea*, Rachel had few financial worries. She returned the last payments of her Guggenheim Fellowship, telling the foundation she no longer needed the funds, and there must be others who did.

In May, Rachel and Bob Hines spent days in the

Florida Keys gathering specimens Rachel wanted drawn. She named three crabs after FWS people they both knew. With her leave of absence almost over, Rachel made a decision. She sent in her resignation. Bob Hines asked how she felt. "Ecstatic!" she said.

Rachel was now free to talk about environmental issues without being bound by the restraints on federal employees. She has been described as only reluctantly political, but she didn't hesitate to express her views

Rachel with Bob Hines in the Florida Keys, 1952.

on issues she cared about. Dwight D. Eisenhower, the newly elected Republican president, set out to change the policy direction of the Department of the Interior. He appointed Douglas McKay, a businessman, as the new secretary. McKay promptly fired Albert Day, director of FWS, and Rachel went public. In a letter to the *Washington Post*, she said Day's dismissal was disturbing, and that it and other staff changes "suggest that the way is being cleared for a raid upon our natural resources that is without parallel within the present century." Day, she said, had stood firm against groups that wanted to "raid these public resources" for private gain. "Hard-won progress is to be wiped out," she concluded, "as a politically minded Administration returns us to the dark ages of unrestrained exploitation and destruction."

In September, Rachel was back in Maine with Bob Hines, gathering material for the seashore book. Sometimes she'd become so stiff wading in the freezing Maine waters, Hines would have to carry her out. These trips were for research, but also served to divert press attention away from Rachel's family. In Washington, Marjie had given birth to Rachel's grandnephew, Roger

Allen Christie. Few of Rachel's friends even knew that Marjie had been pregnant. Some people have said that since Rachel never married, she had little understanding of family responsibilities. In fact she had a lifetime of experience—caring for her parents, siblings, nieces, and grandnephew.

In the midst of family pressures and a new book deadline, Rachel turned down an invitation to join a research expedition to study the effects of radiation from atomic tests in the Pacific islands. The book deadline was her official excuse, but, according to one biographer, "the care of her elderly mother was the deciding factor."

There were more disappointments at the end of 1952. When RKO Studios planned a documentary film of *The Sea Around Us*, Rachel signed a contract she thought gave her control over the material. She was stunned when she read the final script. "Frankly, I could not believe my first reading and had to put it away and then sneak back to it the next day to see if it could possibly be as bad as I thought. But every reading sends my blood pressure higher." The script was filled with errors and was appallingly anthropomorphic. "The practice of attributing human vices and virtues to the lower animals," she said, "went out of fashion many years ago. It persists only at the level of certain Sunday Supplements." But Rachel only had the right to review the material, not the power to change it. Some critics said the film bore no relation to the book. Still, it won an Academy Award in 1953 for best documentary, only confirming Rachel's wariness of popular media.

For the first half of 1953, Rachel struggled to find the right approach to the seashore book. As she later said,

The writer must never attempt to impose himself upon his subject. He must not try to mold it according to what he believes his readers or editors want to read. His initial task is to come to know his subject intimately, to understand its every aspect, to let it fill his mind. Then at some turning point the subject takes command and the true act of creation begins. . . . The discipline of the writer is to learn to be still and listen to what his subject has to tell him.

Rachel thought a great deal about the creative process. "The heart of it is something very complex, that has to do with ideas of destiny, and with an almost inexpressible feeling that I am merely the instrument through which something has happened—that I've had little to do with it myself."

In midsummer, Rachel wrote her editor that at last she understood she had been trying "to write the wrong kind of book." She planned now to interpret the different coastal environments—the northern rocky shore, where life is ruled by the tides; the mid-Atlantic sandy beaches, where waves dominate; and the southern coral coastline, where the ocean currents largely determine life forms.

Rachel had fallen in love with the Maine coast. Financially secure for the first time, she bought land on Southport Island near Boothbay Harbor and built a small cottage. "The place overlooks the estuary of the Sheepscot River," she wrote Marie Rodell, "which is very deep, so that sometimes—you'll never guess— *whales* come up past the place, blowing and rolling in all their majesty!" In July, Rachel, her mother, and Muffin, her new cat, moved into the Maine house and met their neighbors, Dorothy and Stanley Freeman. Both Freemans had loved *The Sea Around Us* and were delighted at the prospect of such a renowned author as their neighbor. Dorothy was outgoing, affectionate, and an inveterate letter writer. Nine years older than Rachel, she exuded a warmth and familial stability. She, too, loved Maine, and had spent summers there all her life. And like Rachel, she was taking care of an elderly mother.

Rachel with Dorothy and Stanley Freeman in Maine.

Within a short time, the women were on a first-name basis. Dorothy Freeman, although not a scientist, was an amateur naturalist who deeply appreciated Rachel's science wrapped in poetry. Over the dozen years of their friendship, they spent many more hours writing letters to each other than in actual visits. They wrote about music, poetry, books they were reading, moments in nature, and of their delight in having found a "kindred spirit" in the other. Their letters reflected a loving friendship.*

Rachel met Dorothy at a time of increasing personal stress. "A writer," she wrote her new friend, "is just an ordinary person, and could soon be a very lonely one if his friends started putting him on a pedestal, where he certainly doesn't belong, anyway!"

Mrs. Carson, in her mid-eighties, was often ill, and Marjie, now a single mother, was herself not in good health. Then Muffie, Rachel's cat partner on the new book, died. "I must never have a cat again," she wrote Marie Rodell. "I can't go through this grief again. I had loved the others dearly but Muffie was different."

At last Rachel got back to work. Only in the world of the tide pools and in the vision under her micro-

* See Notes for additional information.

scope did she find a profound sense of joy and contentment. On a research trip to the Florida Keys, she described how she and Shirley Briggs had waited with all their equipment for a bus to the yacht basin. "A stranger who was also waiting for the bus took it all in, then he said to us: 'You girls look as though you were going out to discover a new world.' I think perhaps that remark expressed the keynote of these studies of the shore—the sense of discovery."

In late December 1953, Rachel gave a paper at a conference of the American Association for the Advancement of Science. Unlike her other speeches, it was a strictly scholarly presentation to an academic audience. Four months later in a speech before nearly a thousand women journalists, Rachel spoke more autobiographically than she had ever before or would again. She talked about her childhood and her longing for the sea. She spoke of her early desire to be a writer and the seeming conflict when she discovered her love of science. She told amusing stories about her job with the Bureau of Fisheries, the voyage with Marie Rodell on the *Albatross*, and her expeditions with Shirley Briggs. She regaled the audience with understated but pointed stories of some male responses to her work.

In a more serious vein she said, "There is one quality that characterizes all of us who deal with the sciences of the earth and its life—we are never bored. We can't be. There is always something new to be investigated. Every mystery solved brings us to the threshold of a greater one." "We are never bored"—that, in a phrase, probably reveals as much as anything the intellectual essence of Rachel Carson. At the end of her speech, Rachel said,

> I am not afraid of being thought a sentimental-
> ist when I stand here tonight and tell you that
> I believe natural beauty has a necessary place in
> the spiritual development of any individual or
> any society. I believe that whenever we destroy
> beauty, or whenever we substitute something
> man-made and artificial for a natural feature of
> the earth, we have retarded some part of man's
> spiritual growth.

She concluded, "But I believe that the more clearly we can focus our attention on the wonders and realities of the universe about us, the less taste we shall have for destruction." The organizers of the conference told her it was the best speech ever presented to the group.

In mid-June, Rachel was thrilled to learn that the *New Yorker* was interested in serializing the seashore book, now called *The Edge of the Sea*. Editor William Shawn told Marie, "She's done it again." Rachel's respect for Shawn was enormous, and such an accolade from him quieted her fears that she'd never match her work in *The Sea Around Us*.

Rachel gave one more speech at the end of December. Then she returned to her writing. It must have been hard for her to imagine working without a cat. Buzzie and Kito had helped with *Under the Sea-Wind*, Tippy with *The Sea Around Us*, and Muffie had been there at the start of *The Edge of the Sea*. Now Jeffie joined the pantheon of feline collaborators. By mid-March Rachel had completed most of the book.

"What a wonderful woman you are!" her editor wrote. "I am convinced that [the manuscript] contains some of the best writing you have ever done and that there are passages here superior to anything in *The Sea Around Us*." Rachel met the staff of Houghton Mifflin at a sales conference. In the new book, she said, "I am telling something of the story of how that marvelous, tough, vital, and adaptable something we know as LIFE has come to occupy one part of the sea world and how it has adjusted itself and survived despite the immense, blind forces acting upon it from every side."

Rachel had loved the research, spending time in the low-tide world, watching flame-colored anemones swaying as they reached for food, observing tiny sea creatures go about their lives. "When the ebb tide falls very early in the morning, and the world is full of salt-smell, and the sound of water, and the softness of fog"—those were the moments Rachel treasured. The public seemed to treasure them, too. Within weeks, the book was on both the *New York Herald Tribune* and the *New York Times* best seller lists, and remained on the *Times* list for twenty-three weeks. One explanation, Rachel wrote her editor, was that "people are fascinated by the thought that sand is not just sand."

Some reviewers said they missed the broad, cosmic scale of *The Sea*. Others appreciated the splendor Carson had found in a grain of sand. In the preface, Rachel evoked a theme from her childhood:

To understand the life of the shore, it is not enough to pick up an empty shell and say "This is a murex," or "That is an angel wing." True under-standing demands intuitive comprehension of the whole life of the creature that once inhabited this empty shell; how it survived amid surf and storms, what were its enemies, how it found food and reproduced its kind, what were its relations to the particular sea world in which it lived.

The *New York Times* reviewer echoed William Shawn's comment. "The main news about Miss Carson is that she has done it again. Her new book is as wise and wonderful as 'The Sea Around Us.'"

TEN

Under the Name of Civilization

RACHEL TOOK COMFORT in the fact that she wasn't a flash-in-the-pan in the eyes of the public. She was tired, satisfied, and found it "a luxury just to read, and not to try to write." While working on *The Edge*, however, she had agreed to write a book about evolution. "I am really laughing at myself," she wrote Dorothy, "for even supposing I could take any appreciable 'time off' before beginning the new book." But in fact she was happy. "I am taking to this research like an old alcoholic to his bottle. . . . I find my mind in a ferment of ideas."

Smaller projects with more immediate deadlines, however, took precedence. Producers of the CBS television program *Omnibus* had film footage of clouds and asked Rachel to write an accompanying script. She didn't own a television, but curiosity about both clouds and the new medium clinched the deal. The idea had come from an eight-year-old girl who'd written to CBS, "Will you please put on your show something about the sky. I have herd [sic] so much about the sky."

The producers gave Rachel free rein, and she in turn asked viewers to see more than the obvious:

> Hidden in the beauty of the moving clouds is a story that is as old as the earth itself. The clouds are the writing of the wind on the sky. They carry the signature of masses of air drifting across sea and land. They are the aviator's promise of good flying weather, or an omen of furious turbulence hidden within their calm exterior. But most of all they are cosmic symbols, representing an age-old process that is linked with life itself.

The show aired on March 11, 1956. Rachel watched it at her brother's home and bought a television days later.

Over the years, several publications had wanted to interview Rachel, but she routinely refused, in the name of privacy. She was willing to share her work, not her personal life. But when the *Woman's Home Companion* editors suggested an article helping parents to introduce their children to the world of nature, she agreed. "The *Companion* editors," she wrote a friend, "true to editorial habits of thought, wish me to 'personalize' (horrid word!) the piece as much as possible in terms of Roger." She permitted only one photograph of him. Rachel planned to turn the piece into a book, but she never did.*

Rachel's circle of friends had widened with the publication of *The Edge of the Sea*. Curtis Bok, an author and Pennsylvania judge, was an avid correspondent. "I have, as you may have observed, an undisciplined pen," he wrote. Undisciplined, perhaps, but insightful and engaging. Rachel wrote Bok that she wasn't certain how to approach the subject of evolution. It was "boggy ground," he replied.

"I hope I can find a path that skirts around it on firmer ground," she answered. "As a biologist, I shall indeed try to stick to what we can observe and test— always realizing, of course, that what we do know now is only a tiny fragment of what Really Is!"

* See Notes for additional information.

"Yes, Rachel," he wrote, "face up to it like a big brave girl: what are you going to do about God?"

Rachel accepted an award for outstanding scholarship from the American Association of University Women, and in her speech she touched on the "boggy ground." "I had been one of those who believed we should never be able to penetrate the mystery of how life arose. Now, studying the work of some modern pioneers in biochemistry, I have come to believe science can at least form a reasonable theory to account for that mystery of all mysteries."

Rachel also talked about writing, a "lonely occupation at best," she said.

Of course there are stimulating and even happy associations with friends and colleagues, but during the actual work of creation the writer cuts himself off from all others and confronts his subject alone. He moves into a realm where he has never been before—perhaps where no one has ever been. It is a lonely place, and even a little frightening.

There were times Rachel might have preferred more "loneliness." Her mother, in her late eighties, was increasingly frail, and her niece Marjie was often sick, leaving Rachel to take care of Roger. Rachel had been paying Marjie's rent and helping with hospital bills, and so she began looking for a larger house with room for Marjie and Roger. "What is needed," she wrote Dorothy, "is a near-twin of me who can do everything I do except write, and let me do that!"

In Maine for the summer, Rachel had a new project. She hoped to buy and preserve a stretch of forest on the

Rachel (center) with niece Marjie and grandnephew Roger.

coast that she and Dorothy called the "Lost Woods."
She wrote Bok, "When, a few years back and for the
first time in my life, money somewhat beyond actual
needs began to come to me . . . I felt that, almost above
all else, I wished some of the money might go . . . to
furthering these things I so deeply believe in." To raise
money for her land-buying dream, that fall she agreed
to oversee a juvenile version of *The Sea* and compile a
comprehensive anthology of nature writings.

One evening that summer, Rachel and Marjie stood
on her Maine beach mesmerized by the swell of the surf
and the brilliance of the phosphorescence.* Droplets
of water glittered like diamonds and emeralds. When
a shimmering spark flew past them, Rachel realized it
was a firefly.

He was flying so low over the water that his light
cast a long surface reflection, like a little headlight.
Then the truth dawned on me. He "thought" the
flashes in the water were other fireflies, signaling
to him in the age-old manner of fireflies! Sure
enough, he was soon in trouble and we saw his
light flashing urgently as he was rolled around

* See Notes for additional information.

in the wet sand—no question this time which was insect and which the unidentified little sea will-o-the-wisps!

Rachel rescued him and put him in a bucket to dry out his wings. She described the event to a scientist friend, who wrote back, "The observation is most interesting and should be published—perhaps in *Science*—as a short note." He added that this was the first report he'd heard of fireflies attracted to the light of a sea creature, but, trusting Rachel as a scientist, "it is undoubtedly the case from your experience."

Back in Maryland, Rachel hired a full-time housekeeper. Ida Sprow, who made a fine impression when Jeffie leapt on her lap during her interview, began to work for the Carsons in the late fall.

The new year, anticipated so happily, began with a series of minor illnesses. When Roger had a fever, Rachel told Marie it was tough to keep a five-year-old in bed, when he was "lively as 17 crickets." Then Marjie was hospitalized with pneumonia. Shirley Briggs talked with Rachel. "We recalled our Florida trip and she said it was hard to imagine being that carefree again ever."

Rachel told Dorothy, "The possibility of working or even writing a letter, no matter how urgent—has been at least as remote as a personal trip to the moon." Then, just when Rachel thought Marjie was improving, her thirty-one-year-old niece died. Roger was five; Rachel, fifty; and Maria Carson, eighty-eight.

Rachel adopted Roger. "He had lost his father before he could remember him," she wrote Paul Brooks, "and in our small family I am the logical one to care for him and . . . the one who is really closest to him." Rachel bought land in Silver Spring, Maryland, and planned to build a house for her remaining family.

Then a long-time Carson family friend, Alice Mullen, died. "Not often in one's whole lifetime does one find a real kindred spirit," Rachel wrote Dorothy. "In their different ways, both Alice and Marjie were that to me, and in an interval of less than three months they have both gone." Distracted by grief and burdened with responsibilities, Rachel was unable to do much work. The anthology idea was shelved, along with the Lost Woods dream. The price for the seacoast property was more than she could afford.

The outside world seemed equally bleak. Rachel

was deeply troubled by the rapid pace of technological change that seemed to threaten all she treasured. In the fall of 1957, the Soviet Union sent the first satellites, Sputnik I and II, into outer space. "What a strange future we all have to face!" she wrote Dorothy. "It seems to me all I have ever said or believed has lost much of its meaning in the light of recent events." At first she rejected "unattractive" ideas, for nature, surely, would survive man's tampering:

He might level the forests and dam the streams, but the clouds and the rain and the wind were God's. . . . These beliefs have almost been part of me for as long as I have thought about such things. . . . To have them even vaguely threatened was so shocking that . . . I shut my mind—refused to acknowledge what I couldn't help seeing. But that does no good, and I have now opened my eyes and my mind. I may not like what I see, but it does no good to ignore it, and it's worse than useless to go on repeating the old "eternal verities" that are no more eternal than the hills of the poets. So it seems time someone wrote of Life in the light of the truth as it now appears to us. And I think that may be the book I am to write.

First she took on a small project, an article for *Holiday* magazine, about wild beach coasts. "In every outthrust headland, in every curving beach, in every grain of sand there is a story of the earth," she wrote. Once, walking through early morning mists, she had reached the water's edge. "For all one could tell the time might have been Paleozoic, when the world was in very fact only rocks and sea."

She shared her sense of excitement and awe, and then she issued a wake-up call. Some of the places she'd written about were no longer pristine. "Instead, they have been tainted by the sordid transformation of 'development'—cluttered with amusement concessions, refreshment stands, fishing shacks—all the untidy litter of what passes under the name of civilization." Above the din of man, the voice of the sea, she wrote, can no longer be heard. She made a plea for preserving wilderness areas. "Somewhere we should know what was Nature's way; we should know what the earth would have been had not man interfered. . . . For there remains, in this space-age universe, the possibility that man's way is not always best."

There were other alarming events. In the 1940s, Rachel and her colleagues at FWS had questioned the indiscriminate use of DDT. Now, more than ten years later, one of the Agriculture Department's weapons of choice in its "war" on the fire ant was DDT. The Department planned to spray twenty million acres in the South and Southwest with toxic chemicals, including DDT. The government launched a public relations campaign with press releases, films, and planted "news" stories. Without a national environmental movement, few people knew of the dangers of pesticides. Most thought of these chemicals only as allies in the battle against pests.

Some critics accused the USDA of overkill. With cutting humor, the executive director of the National Wildlife Federation suggested that using massive amounts of toxic pesticides was like "the cure for dandruff which involves scalping the patient."

Some citizens fought back. In U.S. Federal Court in New York, a group of Long Islanders filed a lawsuit to stop federal and state spraying of their land. The "enemy" this time was the gypsy moth. In the upcoming trial, evidence would be submitted about the damage to birds and "good" insects, while at the same time some real pests were developing resistance to the chemicals. There also would be testimony about hazards to human health.

Then Rachel's friend Olga Owens Huckins sent her the letter she'd written to the *Boston Herald*. Huckins described the poisoning of birds in her own bird sanctuary that had resulted from aerial spraying to kill mosquitoes. Her songbirds had "died horribly," and the mosquitoes were worse than ever.

Huckins's letter, Rachel wrote, "brought my attention sharply back to a problem with which I had long been concerned."

ELEVEN
Reverence for Life

RACHEL PLUNGED INTO research on pesticides. She was in touch with former government colleagues, naturalists, doctors, the plaintiffs in the Long Island lawsuit, and scientists all over the world. She didn't believe you could "contain" pollution. If you spray trees to get rid of the gypsy moth, leaves fall, worms eat the leaves, and birds eat the worms. Some birds then lay eggs with shells so fragile they crack; some birds can't reproduce at all; many die.

Marjorie Spock, one of the Long Island plaintiffs, became a friend. She was comfortable with kids, and now that Rachel was responsible for Roger, that was important. Marjorie sent Roger games and books she thought he'd like. And she sent Rachel articles about pesticides, the trial transcript, and lists of contacts.

The more Rachel learned, the more she realized she

wanted to write about the irresponsible use of toxic chemicals. So much was at stake—the health of the environment and the well-being of humans. Perhaps she could do an article that would be a chapter in a short book. Marie Rodell agreed, but couldn't interest any magazines. One fear was obvious—the loss of advertising from companies that sold pesticides. Rachel wrote Paul Brooks at Houghton Mifflin and William Shawn at the *New Yorker* about her ideas. Both were interested. Shawn wanted a long two-part article for the magazine, and Rachel signed a contract with Houghton Mifflin for a book. Shawn said he wanted a piece as tough as she wanted to make it. "After all, there are some things one doesn't have to be objective and unbiased about—one doesn't condone murder!" He added, "We don't usually think of the *New Yorker* as changing the world, but this is one time it might."

With a frail mother and young child at home, Rachel thought she needed a collaborator. Rodell found a science editor at *Newsweek*, but Rachel soon realized that the arrangement would not work. She needed research help, not a coauthor. She hired Bette Haney, a college student, to write summaries of articles.

When Rachel learned that a zoology instructor at the University of California was working on a book about pesticides, she wrote him:

It should cause no concern to either of us, for I learned long ago that it doesn't matter how many people write about the same thing; each will make his own contribution. And I have a feeling that the subject we both have in mind now is an extremely important one for our time, and I welcome the idea that others are dealing with it.

They became good friends and supported each other's work.

Only Dorothy Freeman was not excited about the project. She thought the subject too grim. It pained Rachel that Dorothy didn't understand. "Knowing what I do," Rachel wrote her, "there would be no future peace for me if I kept silent. . . . I wish you could feel, as I do that it is, in the deepest sense, a privilege as well as a duty to have the opportunity to speak out—to many thousands of people—on something so important." Dorothy did eventually come around.

In May 1957, the judge in the Long Island case refused to stop the planned spraying. The court later dismissed the case, saying there was no proof of damages and no plan to repeat the spraying. The plaintiffs appealed, but the Circuit Court ruled against them, saying that since the spraying had already taken place, there was no longer a real problem, only an abstract one, and courts do not deal in abstractions.

Rachel's correspondence was voluminous. She reached out to a broad spectrum of people, anyone with information she felt she could rely on. When she called government offices, nervous officials sometimes hinted at frightening stories—rumors, for example, that a baby food manufacturer was afraid vegetables had been contaminated with pesticides. As is the way with research, one study led to another, one article cited another, one person suggested another.

Rachel immersed herself in books and articles; she spoke with specialists on insects, birds, soil, people, other mammals, marine life. Her sixteen years in government proved invaluable. She knew her way around various governmental libraries, and she knew people. At Marjorie Spock's suggestion, she even contacted hunting and fishing groups. They could be "good allies, and where I still have occasional contacts with writers and organizations of this sort left over from my days in Fish and Wildlife, I am trying to sow more seeds of discontent."

She believed there was "a psychological angle in all this: that people, especially professional men are uncomfortable about coming out against something, especially if they haven't absolute proof the 'something' is wrong, but only a good suspicion. So they will go along with a program about which they privately have acute misgivings." And so she wanted "to build up, in every way I can, the positive alternatives to chemical sprays, for I feel that a book that is wholly against something cannot possibly be as effective as one that points the way to acceptable alternatives."

In late November 1958, Maria Carson, Rachel's first teacher, mentor, helper, and beloved mother had a stroke. Within days she died. "During that last agonizing night," Rachel wrote Dorothy, "I sat most of the time by the bed with my hand slipped under the border of the oxygen tent, holding Mamma's." Rachel stared at the stars, which seemed brighter than she'd ever seen. Her mother "slipped away, her hand in mine. I told Roger about the stars just before Grandma left us, and he said, 'Maybe they were the lights of the angels, coming to take her to heaven.'"

Rachel struggled to deal with her grief and with Roger's loss of his grandmother. She wrote to Marjorie, "More than anyone else I know, she embodied Albert Schweitzer's 'reverence for life.' And while gentle and compassionate, she could fight fiercely against anything she believed wrong, as in our present Crusade! Knowing how she felt about that will help me to return to it soon, and to carry it through to completion."

By mid-January, Rachel was back working. Within a month, she told both Brooks and Shawn that had she done a quick book, it would have been "half-baked, at best. . . . I shall now be able to achieve . . . a synthesis of widely scattered facts, that have not heretofore been considered in relation to each other . . . to build up, step by step, a really damning case against the use of these chemicals as they are now inflicted upon us." The "really damning case," she thought, was the evidence of perils to human health.

Rachel understood the explosive nature of her research. When she was asked to speak at a National Wildlife Federation conference, she declined. "I may seem unduly cautious, but from all I know of the extremely powerful pressures that can be applied and from advice given me by those in position to know, I think it wise to keep my project under wraps just as long as possible."

Rachel had to be careful. The Department of Agriculture had ties to the chemical industry. Some of her contacts with government personnel now had a cloak and dagger quality, worthy of a thriller novel. Rachel found people willing to help only so long as she never revealed their names.

In April Rachel went public with a letter to the *Washington Post*. She quoted a leading British ecologist who had described "'an amazing rain of death upon the surface of the earth.' . . . The key," Rachel explained, "to the decimation of the robins, which in some parts of the country already amounts to virtual extinction is their reliance on earthworms as food." She wrote, "To many of us, this sudden silencing of the song of birds, this obliteration of the color and beauty and interest of bird life, is sufficient cause for sharp regret." But everyone should pay attention, for "if this 'rain of death' has produced so disastrous an effect on birds, what of other lives, including our own?"

Scientists and doctors Rachel worked with believed there was a medical connection between DDT exposure and effects on the health of people. Rachel also collected individuals' stories. In one letter, a sportsman had written that on a hunting trip in August 1957 he had sprayed his tent for three weeks with DDT.

We did not sufficiently aerate the tent. When I got back home in September, my marrow and white and red corpuscles were terribly impaired. I nearly lost my life. I have had forty-one infusions in my arm, each lasting from four to six to eight hours, in Philadelphia, and I am slowly coming back.

At the bottom of the letter Rachel wrote, "Died of leukemia, May 1959."

Then there was America's national symbol. A front-page *New York Times* headline read "U.S. Is Losing Its Bald Eagles; Sterility Suspected, DDT Cited." A Florida study showed that 80 percent of the bald eagles in that state were sterile. They dined on fish, which had large residues of DDT in their bodies.

By November, when Americans were sitting down to give thanks, the "cranberry scare" of 1959 exploded in the headlines. Scientific studies showed that the herbicide aminotriazole, approved by the USDA, caused cancer of the thyroid in laboratory rats. The Food and Drug Administration (FDA) banned the sale of cranberries that had been sprayed with the herbicide. At a

DDT spraying at Jones Beach, New York, 1945.

public hearing, a Tufts University doctor testified for the industry, arguing that the chemical was harmless. He used it, he said, in treating patients with thyroid conditions. "Oh dear—" Rachel wrote Dorothy, "his testimony can be shot so full of holes as to be absolutely worthless, and the disheartening thing is that he must know this full well, if he is the great specialist they say he is."

The cranberry scare wasn't the only frightening event. During the 1950s, strontium-90, a radioactive substance, was released into the atmosphere as a result of nuclear weapons testing. Dispersed through rainfall, it entered the food chain. In 1959, *Consumer Reports* magazine published an article about strontium-90 in the U.S. diet, particularly in milk. The health risks were frightening—bone cancer and leukemia.

Rachel was writing for a public that knew about atomic fallout. In 1946 the *New Yorker* had turned over all its pages to a report called "Hiroshima." Shortly after the United States dropped atomic bombs on the Japanese cities of Hiroshima and Nagasaki at the end of World War II, reporter John Hersey went to Japan to interview survivors. He told the stories of six people in unemotional language—six ordinary people like the magazine's readers. The issue sold out the moment it hit the newsstands. "Hiroshima" was serialized on the radio, and the Book-of-the-Month Club gave free copies to all its members. It was published as a book and has never gone out of print. Rachel drew the obvious comparison between radiation poisoning and pesticide poisoning.

The writing, as always, was slow. Rachel had planned to complete the book by the end of the year, but that was clearly not possible. When her assistant went back to school, Rachel hired Jeanne Davis as a part-time researcher, secretary, and general assistant. Davis became a friend as well.

"I know it has been hard on everyone's nerves to take so long," Rachel wrote Marjorie Spock, "but I feel in the end it will be very much better to have done so." And to Dorothy she said, "This may well outweigh in importance everything else I have done."

With the start of 1960, Rachel was felled by a number of illnesses—an ulcer, pneumonia, and then a sinus infection. "So now I live on baby foods, Maalox, and Probanthine for a while," she wrote Marie Rodell. "It's a horrid nuisance, but otherwise I'm not concerned."

At last back on track, she wrote Paul Brooks that her research on cancer in humans had expanded.

Then Rachel discovered cysts in her breast. Because of her earlier history, she was scheduled for surgery. After the operation, a radical mastectomy, Rachel specifically asked if the tumors were cancerous. The doctor said no, the surgery had been preventative, and recommended no further treatment. Rachel told only a few friends. "I suppose it's a futile effort to keep one's private affairs private," she wrote Marjorie Spock. "Somehow I have no wish to read of my ailments in literary gossip columns." Rachel's recovery was slow and painful. She wrote in bed when she could. Bette Haney returned from school, and Rachel rehired her. One day Haney interviewed a USDA official who abruptly ended the meeting when he learned she was working for Rachel Carson. The official had looked very nervous, Haney reported. "He should be," Rachel said, and found another source.

Years later Haney said she never thought Rachel would finish the book.

It was not because of all the obvious difficulties; her illness, her mother's death, care of Roger, but more with the pace of work . . . it seemed so slow. As a child of my culture, I had not yet learned to associate progress with that pace . . . and I did not know then the extent of her determination and what a powerful force that kind of determination can be.

Rachel was meticulous. "I do know from my own experience that one cannot accept any statement from whatever source as truth, until one takes the time to trace it to its original source." She knew, for example, that the USDA had tried to have a number of biologists working in federal and state agencies fired because they had questioned the Department's pesticide programs. But she didn't use the story when she couldn't get "copies of letters that prove it."

In the spring, the United States Supreme Court refused to hear the appeal in the Long Island spraying case. Justice William O. Douglas dissented,* and in a sharply worded opinion said that the issues were of great public importance. He quoted at length from Carson's *Washington Post* letter, and *Saturday Review* magazine reprinted his dissent in full. Rachel, still

* See Notes for additional information.

searching for a title for the book, wondered if *Dissent in Favor of Man* was any good. Brooks didn't like it. But with all the talk about dead robins, he suggested "Silent Spring" might be the title for the chapter about pesticides and birds. Later both he and Marie Rodell suggested it as the title for the whole book. Rachel wasn't sure.

During the summer and fall of 1960, Rachel worked for the John F. Kennedy presidential campaign. The Eisenhower administration had been a disaster, in her opinion, on environmental issues. She hoped Democrats would talk about pollution from both chemical and radioactive sources. When Kennedy won the election, Rachel was invited to attend a special inaugural event. Roger, nearly eight years old, was very impressed.

In November, Rachel stopped work. She felt a lump between ribs on the side of her last operation. The doctors said she should have a series of radiation treatments. Then, without further explanation, they recommended chemotherapy. What hadn't they told her, she wondered. She wrote to Dr. George Crile, a cancer specialist and friend in Cleveland. "I want to do what must be done, but no more. After all, I still have several books to write, and can't spend the rest of my life in hospitals."

When Dr. Crile requested her medical records, Rachel learned her doctors had lied to her. "Dr. Sanderson did not tell Miss Carson that she had a malignancy," wrote her Maryland doctor. "Because of her being informed that there was no malignancy, her present management is quite difficult." In those years, in addition to public reluctance to talk about cancer, doctors often discussed women's cancers only with their husbands. That Rachel had asked a direct question made no difference. She was a single woman who did not get a straight answer from her doctor. She told Paul Brooks the cancer had spread and added, "I was told none of this, even though I asked directly."

Dr. Crile was straightforward. "I appreciate," Rachel wrote him, "your having enough respect for my mentality and emotional stability to discuss all this frankly with me. I have a great deal more peace of mind when I feel I know the facts, even though I might wish they were different."

Rachel began radiation treatments back in Washington. She had "a deepened awareness of the preciousness of whatever time is left, be it long or short," she wrote Dorothy, "and a desire to live more affirmatively, making the most of opportunities when they are offered, not putting them off for another day." She worried about Roger. "If it must be that his world has to be shattered again before he reaches manhood, at least I want while there is time to share as many 'wonders' as possible with him."

At the beginning of 1961, Rachel was confined to her bed or a wheelchair, and was in and out of the hospital. One day she was, "so indescribably weak and ill . . . I just had the feeling that at that moment life had burned down to a very tiny flame, that might so easily flicker out." Her plans to complete the book by March were, of course, shattered.

Rachel treasured every glimpse of spring—the return of birds to her yard, the croaking of frogs, the pushing up of crocuses through the thawing earth. "All these reminders that the cycles and rhythms of nature are still at work," she wrote, "are so satisfying." Her letters to friends reported on the doings of her little family—updates on Roger, his school triumphs, his colds, his loneliness, his adventures; and reports on the antics of Jeffie and Moppet.

She worked when she could, sending completed sections to her editor. She and Paul and Marie continued to search for a title. They tried out "The War Against Nature" and "At War with Nature," neither to anyone's liking. Marie joked it should be called "Carson: Opus #4."

When Roger's school let out, Bob Hines drove Rachel, Roger, and the cats to Maine. The few visitors who came that summer were all comfortable with kids, and Roger, a lonely little boy, thrived on the company. By August, Rachel was nearly finished. Revision lay ahead, always a sign the end was in sight. Marie Rodell once again suggested *Silent Spring* as a fitting title. She pointed to the lines from the Keats poem "La Belle Dame Sans Merci":

The sedge is wither'd from the lake,
And no birds sing.

Rachel was convinced.

Always the challenge had been "how to reveal enough to give understanding of the most serious effects of the chemicals without being technical, how to simplify without error—these have been problems of rather monumental proportions." And overall, how to convey the idea that there is a constant interaction between living things and their environment.

The research was massive; the work, monumental; that Rachel completed it in her condition, extraordinary. Her last task was to write the first chapter, "A Fable for Tomorrow." She wrote of a town "in the heart of America where all life seemed to live in harmony with its surroundings . . . Then a strange blight crept over the area and everything began to change." Death hovered over people as well as animals. Birds vanished; "it was a spring without voices." Streams were lifeless and roadside flowers withered. "No witchcraft, no enemy action had silenced the rebirth of new life in this stricken world. The people had done it themselves." Rachel explained that no single town had experienced all these disasters, but every one of them had happened someplace. Without care, "this imagined tragedy may easily become a stark reality we all shall know."

Rachel spent the end of 1961 virtually blind, with a severe inflammation of the iris, possibly caused by the heavy radiation treatments she had undergone. "Yes, there is quite a story behind *Silent Spring*, isn't there? Such a catalogue of illnesses!" she wrote Dorothy. "If one were superstitious it would be easy to believe in some malevolent influence at work, determined by some means to keep the book from being finished."

About tomorrow and the next day and the next, she felt a great sadness. "But now that it seems I shall somehow make this goal, of course I'm not satisfied—now I want time for the Help Your Child to Wonder book, and for the big Man and Nature book. Then I suppose I'll have others—if I live to be 90 still wanting to say something." As Paul Brooks said, "The calm courage with which she faced all this is hard to exaggerate."

At the end of January, on a Monday night at nine P.M., Rachel's phone rang. "'This is William Shawn,'" the voice said. The book was "'a brilliant achievement'—'you have made it literature' 'full of beauty and loveliness and depth of feeling.'" His reaction meant the world to her. In an uncharacteristically emotional letter, she wrote Dorothy:

You know I have the highest regard for his judgment, and suddenly I knew from his reaction that my message would get across. After Roger was asleep I took Jeffie into the study and played the Beethoven violin concerto—one of my favorites, you know. And suddenly the tensions of four years were broken and I got down and put my arms around Jeffie and let the tears come. With his little warm, rough tongue he told me that he understood. I think I let you see last summer what my deeper feelings are about this when I said I could never again listen happily to a thrush song if I had not done all I could. And last night the thoughts of all the birds and other creatures and all the loveliness that is in nature came to me with such a surge of deep happiness, that now I *had* done what I could—I had been able to complete it—now it had its own life!

TWELVE

An Argument with a Woman

"I WANT TO warn you that I am convinced you are going to be subjected to ridicule and condemnation by a few," a former colleague wrote Rachel. "Facts will not stand in the way of some confirmed pest control workers and those who are receiving substantial subsidies from pesticides manufacturers."

But how to prepare for that onslaught? Rachel and Marie thought that if advance copies of *Silent Spring* could be placed in the hands of prominent, sympathetic readers before official publication, some of the criticism might be undercut. They sent copies to congressional staffs, cabinet officials, conservation organizations, women's groups, Supreme Court Justice William O. Douglas, and the White House.

During this flurry of activity, Rachel learned her

cancer had spread. She underwent radiation treatments, and reflected, "if only I could set the calendar back two years. . . . How differently I would handle it now—how carefully I should select the surgeon. It's hard to see how I could have given so little thought to the possibilities. But there's no use thinking of it now." Her spirits were "rather mercurial," she wrote a friend. "After all it is hard to be either philosophic or courageous when one is feeling sick at one's stomach!" Radiation had taken its toll. When the manuscript went off to the printer, Rachel went off to shop for wigs. With an eye on the absurd and a hand on her pocketbook, she told Dorothy, "I'm in luck, because brown hair is cheapest! Gray is more."

On June 16, the *New Yorker* published the first of its three-part serialization. "Phenomenal!" said a *New Yorker* editor about the amount of mail that poured in. Although a few of the letter writers were critical, most were enthusiastic. A *New York Times* editorial said that Rachel had written a story "few will read without a chill, no matter how hot the weather." The paper anticipated Carson would be "accused of alarmism, or lack of objectivity." But the editors pointed out, "to combat highway carelessness," one doesn't talk about all the drivers who arrived home safely. Besides, Carson did not argue that pesticides should never be used. "She warns of the dangers of misuse and overuse by a public that has become mesmerized by the notion that chemists are the possessors of divine wisdom and that nothing but benefit can emerge from their test tubes."

Rachel escaped to Maine with Roger, the cats, and a stack of fan letters. Marie worried that in the months between the *New Yorker* series and book publication in September, the public would have moved on to the next big news story. But the gods of chance were with Rachel, although at the cost of a grim tale.

In July, two months before the book would come out, the thalidomide scandal broke. Thalidomide was a drug that was widely prescribed in Germany, Britain, and Canada, most often as a sleeping pill, and also to prevent nausea in pregnant women. But Dr. Frances Kelsey of the FDA had prevented it from being sold in the U.S. She wasn't completely comfortable with the "safety studies." Doctors in Europe and Canada were reporting that pregnant women taking the drug had given birth to a startling number of malformed babies.

Thalidomide was pulled off the market, but not before thousands of babies had been born with deformed limbs. The *Washington Post* front page headline read "'Heroine' of FDA Keeps Bad Drug Off Market." President Kennedy awarded Dr. Kelsey a gold medal for distinguished service.

Like the cranberry scare several years before, the thalidomide tragedy once again forced the public to face the dangers of quick-fix chemical "solutions" to problems. When asked to comment by a reporter, Rachel said, "It is all of a piece, thalidomide and pesticides—they represent our willingness to rush ahead and use something new without knowing what the results are going to be."

A week after the *Washington Post* article, a *New York Times* headline read: "'Silent Spring' Is Now Noisy Summer." The article reported that representatives of the $300-million-dollar pesticide industry were accusing Rachel of "crass commercialism." According to the reporter, "A drowsy midsummer has suddenly been enlivened by the greatest uproar in the pesticides industry since the cranberry scare of 1959." A spokesperson for a chemical industry group said they were concerned about "misrepresentation," and planned to spend at least $250,000 to challenge Rachel and the book. The *Times* article said the industry was preparing for a long battle, and concluded that *Silent Spring* had not only created a noisy summer, but "presages a noisy fall."

Lawyers for "giant chemical companies" added to the season's noise by telephoning the *New Yorker* and "brusquely insisting that further installments be cancelled or lawsuits would follow." The *New Yorker*'s lawyer responded to this attempted intimidation by saying, "Everything in those articles has been checked and is true. Go ahead and sue."

When the *New Yorker* couldn't be bullied, the lawyer for the Velsicol Chemical Company, maker of two of the pesticides Rachel talked about, sent a letter to Houghton Mifflin, Rachel's publisher, suggesting that *Silent Spring* might be part of a left-wing conspiracy to undermine Western capitalism. He implied the company might sue if the book was published.

The lawyers at the publishing house were nervous. Rachel feared a lawsuit and the drain on her finances—if you are sued, even if you win, the process costs a great deal of money—but she trusted her facts. And some in the industry agreed with her. "Miss Carson presents facts accurately for the most part," said the review in a chemical and engineering trade journal, quoted in the *New York Times Book Review*, "but comes to unwarranted conclusions from them and ignores the benefits of pesticides." It is hard to sue over an opinion once you have admitted the facts are correct. In the end, no one, not Velsicol nor any other company, ever filed suit against Rachel, Houghton Mifflin, the *New Yorker*, or any group that reprinted part or all of *Silent Spring*.*

In September when the book was published, the attacks on both *Silent Spring* and Rachel herself reached fever pitch. But what was in this book that so aroused fear and rage among its critics?

Rachel had opened with the allegory about a town that was barren of life. It was meant to be a tale with a moral, a series of images to drive, like a line of poetry, straight to the heart of the issue. Then she set forth her ecological premise: "The history of life on earth has been a history of interaction between living things and their surroundings." Everything flowed from that understanding. To introduce chemical poisons into one corner of the environment was to contaminate the rest.

* See Notes for additional information.

"The public must decide whether it wishes to continue on the present road, and it can do so only when in full possession of the facts."

Almost everyone has at one time reached for a spray can to kill a "pest," but few of us have known anything about the ingredients in these products. Rachel described the development of modern pesticides and how they pass through the food chain, then through the human body. Some, many times more poisonous than DDT, are sold as household goods from supermarket shelves.

Rachel wrote of the contamination of lakes, rivers, oceans, and the creatures that live in the world of water. She illustrated the effect on *many* creatures of mass spraying to eliminate *one*. Over and over again she showed how nothing in nature stands alone. In 1955, it was obvious something was terribly wrong in places that had been heavily sprayed the year before to kill elm tree beetles, gypsy moths, and mosquitoes. At Michigan State University, "the campus is serving as a graveyard for most of the robins that attempt to take up residence in the spring," said a professor.

Rachel asked, "Who has made the decision that

sets in motion these chains of poisonings, this ever-widening wave of death that spreads out, like ripples when a pebble is dropped into a still pond? . . . Who has decided—who has the *right* to decide . . . ?" Sometimes, she acknowledged, we have to use pesticides, "but we should do so thoughtfully, with full awareness that what we do may have consequences remote in time and place." She added "no such humility marks the booming 'weed killer' business of the present day, in which soaring sales and expanding uses mark the production of plant-killing chemicals."

Several chapters detailed "The Human Price." The deadly result of accidental overexposure to chemicals was well known. But, Rachel said, we don't yet know the long-term effects resulting from the slow accumulation of toxins in the human body. She cited studies by scientists not beholden to the chemical industry who talked about cancer and possible cellular and genetic mutations from pesticide exposure.

Silent Spring ended on a positive note with a chapter called "The Other Road," in which Rachel explored alternatives. She talked about biological controls, the search for *natural* ways to deal with destructive insects.

One promising technique was to sterilize the males of a species, release them to mate, and thereby prevent reproduction. In other cases, the use of natural predators or plants that displaced intrusive ones eliminated the problems. In the book's final paragraph, Rachel wrote:

> The "control of nature" is a phrase conceived in arrogance, born of the Neanderthal age of biology and philosophy, when it was supposed that nature exists for the convenience of man. The concepts and practices of applied entomology for the most part date from that Stone Age of science. It is our alarming misfortune that so primitive a science has armed itself with the most modern and terrible weapons, and that in turning them against the insects it has also turned them against the earth.

The attack launched by the chemical industry and some government agencies took several forms. Rachel herself was ridiculed as a cat, bird, or fish lover, and a health food faddist. Industry representatives had admitted they could "find little error of fact," and so the president of the Montrose Chemical Corporation, the largest producer of DDT, attacked Rachel herself. Carson wrote, he said, not "as a scientist but rather as a fanatic defender of the cult of the balance of nature." A Federal Pest Control Review Board member reportedly sneered that she was "a spinster. What's she so worried about genetics for?" Others attribute that comment to former Secretary of Agriculture Ezra Taft Benson, written in a letter to Dwight Eisenhower. And Benson, they say, concluded she was "probably a Communist." Benson wasn't the only one to invoke the "red scare." One critic wrote the *New Yorker*:

Miss Rachel Carson's reference to the selfishness of insecticide manufacturers probably reflects her Communist sympathies, like a lot of our writers these days.

We can live without birds and animals, but, as the current market slump shows, we cannot live without business.

As for insects, isn't it just like a woman to be scared to death of a few little bugs! As long as we have the H-bomb everything will be O.K. PS. She's probably a peace-nut too.

Rachel's marital status was a recurrent issue. When a *Baltimore Sun* reporter asked Rachel why she had never married, she said, "No time." She added that she "sometimes envied male writers who married because they had wives to take care of them, provide meals, and spare them from unnecessary interruptions." Rachel was routinely described in personal and physical terms—a petite, soft-spoken spinster. By contrast, her critics, often university scientists with pesticide company affiliations, were described simply as Dr. so-and-so of such-and-such institution.

LIFE magazine in an article called "The Gentle Storm Center," reported on the first page that Carson was not married. The writer described her as "a shy, soft-spoken woman miscast in the role of crusader." The word "miscast" itself misses the essence of Rachel. Yes, she was not one to shout in a loud voice, but once convinced of a position, she used all her skills as a scientist and writer, and all her contacts in the worlds of government, science, and publishing, to argue her position. When Rachel later testified before a Senate committee, one historian wrote:

> Those who heard Rachel Carson that morning did not see a reserved or reticent woman in the witness chair but an accomplished scientist, an expert on chemical pesticides, a brilliant writer, and a woman of conscience who made the most of an opportunity few citizens of any rank can have to make their opinions known. Her witness had been equal to her vision.

Rachel was delighted when she learned that Book of the Month had chosen *Silent Spring* for its October club selection. "BOM," she knew, "will carry it to farms and hamlets all over the country that don't know what a bookstore looks like—much less the *New Yorker*. So it is very, very good and tonight I am deeply and quietly happy."

Until *Silent Spring*, the public barely knew that so-called independent research scientists were on the payroll of chemical companies, and that government agencies, whose employees often came from chemical companies, were dependent on that industry research. "Follow the money trail," investigative reporters say. Rachel did exactly that. In a speech to the Garden Club of America, she said, "As you listen to the present controversy about pesticides, I recommend you ask yourself—Who speaks?—And Why?"

Carson's critics argued that the good outweighed the dangers. Pesticides had kept some harmful insects, other vermin, and certain diseases under control. Moreover, food production would be drastically reduced without pesticides, and people would starve. According to *Time* magazine, "informed people," while recognizing Rachel's writing skills, consider the work "unfair, one-sided, and hysterically overemphatic." And *Time* agreed. "Many of the scary generalizations—and there are lots of them—are patently unsound."

Finally, who was this writer to challenge scientists? critics asked. She wasn't trained, they said, and should stick to her poetry about the ocean. Rachel's editor was mocking in response:

For them should be reserved a special corner in the Library of Hell, equipped with a barnacle-covered bench and a whale-oil lamp, by whose light they would be compelled to read out loud from her master's thesis: "The Development of the Pronephros During the Embryonic and Early Larval Life of the Catfish (*Inctalurus punctatus*)."

Rachel received a letter from E. B. White, thanking her for including a quote of his on the book's epigraph page. He thought *Silent Spring* was like *Uncle Tom's Cabin*, "the sort [of book] that will help turn the tide." That was private correspondence. President Kennedy from a podium in the White House publicly acknowledged the importance of *Silent Spring*. When asked whether government agencies were looking into the dangers of pesticides, he said, "of course, since Miss Carson's book . . . they are examining the matter." The next day the administration announced that a special Presidential committee would review government pesticide programs. Rachel was invited to testify before the committee.

That set the industry scrambling. Fear that the government would impose stringent regulations fueled more attacks. A major industry group distributed a

Rachel (far left), the only woman at President Kennedy's
Science Advisory Committee, 1963.

pamphlet called "How to Answer Rachel Carson."
Monsanto corporation published a parody of Rachel's
fable, called "The Desolate Year," describing a world
without pesticides.

Scientists in universities that received research grants
from chemical firms were on the defensive. A Harvard
Medical School doctor charged that Carson appealed
to emotions. As a demonstration of his own analytic
approach, he called Rachel's conclusions "baloney."

The head of the Department of Biochemistry and a director at Vanderbilt University's School of Medicine, in an equally unemotional look at the book, titled his review "Silence, Miss Carson." Another doctor called the book unscientific, and ended his review on a personal note: "*Silent Spring*, which I read word for word with some trauma, kept reminding me of trying to win an argument with a woman. It can not be done."

On the other hand, according to a doctor at the National Cancer Institute, Rachel was an "unusually well informed scientist," and "when the storm of abuse and denunciation broke, Rachel Carson stood up well against her accusers because her scientific facts were sound and valid and her interpretations were reasonable."

For a person who treasured her privacy, the explosion of publicity was overwhelming. Rachel wrote Shirley Briggs from Maine, "So far I have not had to resort to disguises but I am about to have the telephone changed to an unlisted category, and even with that precaution I think I am about to be invaded by the press."

The book inspired many cartoons. In one, a woman shopper in a garden supply store says to the salesperson,

"Now, don't sell me anything Rachel Carson wouldn't buy." In another, two men stop to look at a dead dog in the street. One says to the other, "This is the dog that bit the cat that killed the rat that ate the malt that came from the grain that Jack sprayed." In still another, a man at a bar says to the bartender, "I had just come to terms with fallout, and along comes Rachel Carson." Even Charles Schultz got into the act with three "Peanuts" cartoons with Rachel as the theme.

In a speech to the National Women's Press Club, Rachel felt it fitting to open with reference to a newspaper article. "My text this afternoon is taken from the *Globe Times* of Bethlehem, Pa." The reporter had described the negative response to *Silent Spring* in two county farm bureaus. "The reporter continued: 'No one in either county farm office who was talked to today had read the book, but all disapproved of it heartily.'"

Many Americans, however, did read the book. One colleague predicted *Silent Spring* "will not be the best seller that *The Sea Around Us* has been. The total effect, however, might be infinitely more important to our national economy and well being." He was wrong and right. *Silent Spring* was number one on the *New York*

Times Best Seller list for most of the fall and again before Christmas 1962, when 106,000 copies were sold in a week. And it is credited with inspiring the environmental movement that continues to engage so many people today.

Silent Spring was also an international best seller. Within a year of publication, the book had provoked a firestorm of interest around the world. A peer in the British House of Lords told of the Polynesian cannibal chief who "no longer allows his tribe to eat Americans because their fat is contaminated with chlorinated hydrocarbons." This was, the peer explained, a matter of "export trade. The figure shows that we are rather more edible than Americans . . . that we have about 2 parts per million of DDT in our bodies, whereas the figure for Americans is about 11 parts per million."

Rachel, battling cancer and often in great pain, turned down most requests for appearances. She did, however, agree to be filmed by CBS Reports. The producer/writer interviewed her in Maine, Maryland, and Washington, D.C. On April 3, 1963, CBS broadcast *The Silent Spring of Rachel Carson*. "What she wrote," the show began, "started a national quarrel." At least half a dozen government officials and industry representatives were interviewed; Rachel was invited to read from the book. She had been ill and in pain most of the time CBS had filmed her. "I just hope I don't look and sound like an utter idiot," she wrote Dorothy. She needn't have worried. She appeared calm, thoughtful, and articulate.

Rachel wasn't just criticizing pesticide misuse. She was challenging the belief that all problems could be solved by technology, and that chemists were gods in this new world. Millions who had not read the book had a chance to see and hear her. "In a single evening, [the CBS] . . . broadcast added the environment to the public agenda," wrote a professor of environmental history. The day after the broadcast Senator Abraham Ribicoff announced he would begin a congressional review of environmental hazards.

On May 15, 1963, the president's special committee reviewing pesticides released its report. The committee largely substantiated Rachel's claims and endorsed a number of her suggestions. CBS did a follow-up program, and Rachel said she felt "vindicated." The show concluded, "Miss Rachel Carson had two immediate aims. One was to alert the public; the second, to build a fire under the Government. She accomplished the first aim months ago. Tonight's report by the Presidential panel is prima facie evidence that she has also accomplished the second."

Rachel on Maine coast.

Epilogue

RACHEL WENT TO Maine in the summer of 1963 for the last time. One morning she and Dorothy sat on a bench overlooking the water. Later that day, Rachel wrote Dorothy. Perhaps it was easier to put the words down on paper than to say them.

But most of all I shall remember the Monarchs, that unhurried westward drift of one small winged form after another, each drawn by some invisible force. We talked a little about their migration, their life history. Did they return? We thought not; for most, at least, this was the closing journey of their lives.

But it occurred to me this afternoon, remembering, that it had been a happy spectacle, that we had felt no sadness when we spoke of the fact that there would be no return. And rightly—for when any living thing has come to the end of its life cycle we accept that end as natural.

For the Monarch, that cycle is measured in a known span of months. For ourselves, the measure is something else, the span of which we cannot know. But the thought is the same: when that intangible cycle has run its course it is a natural and not unhappy thing that a life comes to its end.

That is what those brightly fluttering bits of life taught me this morning. I found a deep happiness in it—so, I hope, may you.

Rachel's cancer continued to spread. As she neared the end of her life, she was honored with more prizes, medals, and invitations to speak in America and abroad. "So many ironic things," she wrote Dorothy. "Now all the 'honors' have to be received for me by someone else." She did travel to California to speak at a major conference about the environment. Marie Rodell went with her, while Jeanne Davis looked after Roger at home. Rachel was brought to the podium in a wheelchair. In her speech she argued that pollution was not simply a problem for science, but a question of morality. What will we leave to future generations?

Rachel had an immediate concern about future generations. What was to become of her beloved Roger, now eleven years old? The child soon would lose his adoptive mother. Then in September Rachel's little cat Moppet died. By mid-December her other cat, Jeffie, was gone. "For exactly three years," she wrote Dorothy, "since I flew to Cleveland in December and first understood my own situation, I have worried about my little family. . . . But oh, I should be glad for Jeffie . . . for it would have been awful for him, and so frightening, if he had survived me. Now that problem exists no more."

There was still the painful question of who would look after Roger. Money was not an issue, for she left an ample trust for him. Two months before she died, she wrote an addition to her will listing her two choices for guardian—Dorothy Freeman's son and his wife, and Paul Brooks and his wife. She had chosen them because each couple had children near Roger's age and "would undertake to rear him with affectionate care in the companionship of their own children." She hoped at least one of the couples would want Roger. Perhaps out of fear they would turn her down, she had not told either one of her wishes. After her death, Roger went to live with Paul Brooks and his wife.

On April 14, 1964, in the late afternoon, Rachel Carson died at home. Senator Ribicoff, conducting a committee review of environmental hazards, opened the day's hearing with these words: "Today we mourn a great lady. All mankind is in her debt."

Nearly fifty years have passed since *Silent Spring* was first published. It became one of the most influential books in the modern world. Rachel Carson had turned a spotlight on environmental issues, and the public demanded action. Old environmental laws were improved and new ones passed. In 1969 Congress enacted the National Environmental Policy Act, which requires federal agencies to consider the environmental impact of every proposed major action, such as road and dam work, forest clearing, the draining of marshlands. Congress also passed the Clean Air Act; Clean Water Act; Insecticide, Fungicide, and Rodenticide Act; Safe Drinking Water Act; Environmental Pesticides Control Act; and the Toxic Substances Control Act. Dozens more laws were passed on the state level. In

1970 President Nixon by executive order established the Environmental Protection Agency (EPA) to consolidate in one agency all the various federal activities regarding environmental protection. On its Web site, the EPA describes *Silent Spring* as an

> exhaustively researched, carefully reasoned, and beautifully written attack on the indiscriminate use of pesticides. . . . *Silent Spring* played in the history of environmentalism roughly the same role that *Uncle Tom's Cabin* played in the abolitionist movement. In fact, EPA today may be said without exaggeration to be the extended shadow of Rachel Carson.

In 1972, DDT was banned for most use in the United States. Within ten years of the ban, the EPA reported that

> such relatively rare birds as the bald eagle, the brown pelican, the osprey and the peregrine falcon are now increasing. A major reason for their comeback is the ban on most uses of the

pesticide DDT. . . . U.S. Fish and Wildlife Service researchers proved that DDE, a breakdown product of DDT, was responsible for the eggshell thinning which caused sharp population declines among certain bird species.

Now, in the twenty-first century, there are more environmental concerns—global warming, destruction of tropical rain forests, overpopulation, depletion of traditional energy resources. And still, problems with pesticides remain. Scarcely a day goes by without a warning about a chemical pollutant and potential environmental consequences. In 2006, the Bureau of Land Management revealed plans to spray weed-killing pesticides over some 932,000 acres covering parts of seventeen states. Because of Rachel Carson and the environmental movement she inspired, however, the public knows much more than it did in 1962. Environmental organizations are now quick to respond, mobilizing public opinion to pressure Congress and filing lawsuits to challenge government and private actions they believe degrade the environment. The battle is in the hands of each new generation, for Rachel's vision is as relevant and her warnings as urgent today as they ever were.

Although a seeming departure from her earlier books celebrating the natural world, *Silent Spring* was true to all Rachel believed. She warned of ecological death and destruction *because* she wanted to preserve the natural world and let each new generation share in the sense of wonder she so passionately felt.

Paul Brooks, her editor, has described the single most revealing moment in his long friendship with Rachel. One night in Maine when she was working on *The Edge of the Sea*, they had spent a long time looking through her microscope at tiny marine creatures. At last they were finished.

Then, pail and flashlight in hand, she stepped carefully over the kelp-covered rocks to return the living creatures to their home. This, I think, is what Albert Schweitzer . . . meant by "reverence for life." In one form or another it lies behind everything that Rachel Carson wrote.

Notes

FOREWORD:

"patently unsound": *Time*, September 28, 1962.

"Before there was . . .": *Time*, March 29, 1999.

"Every once in . . .": Senator Ernest Gruening, June 4, 1963, 88th Congress (1 sess.), 220–21.

INTRODUCTION:

"Mr. President, there . . . Miss Carson's book . . .": Brooks, *The House of Life*, 305.

CHAPTER ONE

"dear, plump, little . . . very good.": Lear, *Witness*, 15.

"Carson's Grove": Rachel Carson Homestead, www.rachelcarsonhomestead.org.

"solitary child . . . happiest . . .": Lear, *Witness*, 16.

"I can remember . . ." and "I read a . . .": Carson, *Lost Woods*, 148.

"child's playground; where . . .": Lear, *Witness*, 18.

"this story was . . .": Lear, *Witness*, 7.

"I doubt that . . .": Brooks, *The House of Life*, 16.

"Soon our trail . . .": *St. Nicholas League*, July, 1922. The full piece is reprinted in Carson, *Lost Woods*, 13.

"Intellectual Dissipation . . . thoughts of others": The Lear/Carson Collection.

"good-humored": Lear, *Witness*, 493 n. 55.

CHAPTER TWO

*In 1955, Pennsylvania College for Women changed its name to Chatham College.

"Who I Am . . . a heaven for?'" Rachel Carson Collection. The quote, "But a man's reach . . ." is from Browning's poem, "Andrea del Sarto." It was probably written from memory for Rachel used the word "must" whereas Browning wrote "should."

"Well, I could . . .": "I Remember Rachel," Margaret Fifer, née Wooldridge, Rachel Carson Collection.

"'bragged on' Rachel . . . the commuter": Margaret Fifer, née Wooldridge, Rachel Carson Collection. See also Lear, *Witness*, 30–31.

"girl on whom . . . after professional care": Margaret Fifer, née Wooldridge, Rachel Carson Collection.

"His philosophy, humor . . .": "Who I Am," Rachel Carson Collection.

"wasn't anti-social . . . to do it": Sterling, *Sea and Earth*, 43.

"long lazy swells . . . for miles": *The Englicode*, printed in *The Arrow*, April 30, 1926.

"so reserved and . . . self-containmnent": "How I remember Rachel," Dorothy Thompson Seif, Rachel Carson Collection.

"I love all . . .": "Who I Am," Rachel Carson Collection.

"I have gone dead! . . .": Lear, *Witness*, 39.

"You think I . . .": "Why I Am a Pessimist," *The Arrow*, November 19, 1926, Rachel Carson Collection.

"On a night when . . . with the sea.": Freeman, *Always, Rachel*, 59.

"Broken Lamps": *The Englicode*, printed in *The Arrow*, May 27, 1927, Rachel Carson Collection.

CHAPTER THREE

"Butterfly poised on . . .": *The Arrow*, January 13, 1928, Rachel Carson Collection.

"We settled back . . .": Sterling, *Sea and Earth*, 54.

"baggy blue bloomers . . .": Seif, op.cit., Rachel Carson Collection.

"She turned out . . .": Fifer, op.cit., Rachel Carson Collection.

"Extras—Two goats . . .": *The Arrow*, December 16, 1927, Rachel Carson Collection.

"I've gotten bawled . . .": Letter to Mary Frye, March 6, 1928, courtesy of The Lear/Carson Collection.

"Anyone who can . . .": Fifer, op.cit., Rachel Carson Collection.

"I sing of trays . . .": *The Arrow*, March 9, 1928, Rachel Carson Collection.

"That was one . . .": Letter, February 22, 1928, Rachel Carson Collection, courtesy of The Lear/Carson Collection.

"a glorious time": Lear, *Witness*, 44. See also p. 497 n. 56.

"In lots of . . ." "To be engrossed . . ." and "It must be . . .": Lear, *Witness*, 47.

"would just as . . .": Lear, *Witness*, 48.

"a farce" and "You can never . . .": Lear, *Witness*, 49.

"Rachel Carson '29": *The Arrow*, April 22, 1929, Rachel Carson Collection.

"I didn't care . . .": Lear, *Witness*, 52.

"A muse of fire . . .": PCW yearbook, Rachel Carson Collection.

"Rachel, I want you . . .": Lear, *Witness*, 53.

CHAPTER FOUR

"The [boat] trip over . . .": Letter to Dorothy Thompson, August

4, 1929, Rachel Carson Collection, courtesy of The Lear/Carson Collection.

"at sea": Lear, *Witness*, 58.

"began storing away . . ." and "One can't walk . . .": Lear, *Witness*, 60.

"adding to our . . ." "Nothing has ever . . ." and "You may be glad . . .": Letter, August 25, 1929, Rachel Carson Collection, courtesy of The Lear/Carson Collection.

"I was never . . .": Lear, *Witness*, 67.

"the terror of . . . of many there": Lear, *Witness*, 68.

"The professors are . . .": Lear, *Witness*, 67.

"the lab is . . .": Lear, *Witness*, 66.

"lovely woods at . . .": Lear, *Witness*, 67.

"kind woman. . . . She . . .": Lear, *Witness*, 71.

"It's a pretty up-hill . . . you're an Amazon": Lear, *Witness*, 70.

"the squirrels would . . .": Lear, *Witness*, 72.

"of considerable worry . . . no better prospects.": Letter to Miss Margaret Stuart, February 27, 1931, Rachel Carson Collection.

"I learned something . . .": Lear, *Witness*, 72.

"excellent review of . . . point of view.": Lear, *Witness*, 74.

"Deep and sincere . . .": Letter to Miss Margaret Stuart, August 26, 1932, Rachel Carson Collection.

CHAPTER FIVE

"Romance under the . . . fish tales.": Lear, *Witness*, 78

"I've never seen . . ." and "I had given . . .": April 21, 1954, speech to Theta Sigma Phi, the national fraternity for women in journalism, in Carson, *Lost Woods*, 149.

"I am glad . . .": Lear, *Witness*, 83.

"If this favorite . . .": *Baltimore Sunday Sun*, March 1, 1936, Lear, *Witness*, 79.

"largely with economic . . .": Lear, *Witness*, 87.

"My chief read . . .": Carson, *Lost Woods*, 150.

"We have everyone . . .": Lear, *Witness*, 86–87.

"Who has known . . .": *Atlantic Monthly*, September 1937, 322.

"At last comes . . .": *Atlantic Monthly*, September 1937, 323.

"Every living thing . . .": *Atlantic Monthly*, September 1937, 325.

"From those four . . .": April 21, 1954, speech to Theta Sigma Phi, in Carson, *Lost Woods*, 150.

"enjoyed the undersea . . . in my head": Carson, *Lost Woods*, 55. Both quotes are from Carson's "Memo to Mrs. Eales" in the publisher's marketing department, explaining how she came to write the book.

"Maybe Jules Verne . . .": Lear, *Witness*, 88. Bracketed addition is Lear's. Van Loon's *The Story of Mankind* was read by both adults and children, and won the first Newbery Medal, given in 1922.

"Most people stay . . . blowing sand": Carson, *Lost Woods*, 56–57.

"The first chill . . . cold water.": Carson, *Under the Sea-Wind*, 79–81.

"Of course . . . I . . .": Freeman, *Always, Rachel*, 281.

"For three centuries . . .": Lear, *Witness*, 92.

"It has been . . .": Lear, *Witness*, 93.

"I was getting . . .": Brooks, *The House of Life*, 32.

"From that time . . .": "Memo to Mrs. Eales," in Carson, *Lost Woods*, 55.

CHAPTER SIX

"I was delighted . . .": Brooks, *The House of Life*, 4.

"My constant companions . . . for a nap.": Brooks, *The House of Life*, 33.

"determined to avoid . . .": "Memo to Mrs. Eales," in Carson, *Lost Woods*, 55.

"as biographies usually . . .": "Memo to Mrs. Eales," in Carson, *Lost Woods*, 58.

"This ceaseless ebb . . .": "Memo to Mrs. Eales," in Carson, *Lost Woods*, 59.

"by counting the . . .": "Memo to Mrs. Eales," in Carson, *Lost Woods*, 61.

"Time measured by . . ." and "We must not . . .": Carson's emphasis. Carson, *Under the Sea-Wind*, xvi–xvii, first edition.

"The smell of . . .": "Memo to Mrs. Eales," in Carson, *Lost Woods*, 56.

"It seems to me . . .": Lear, *Witness*, 102.

"There is poetry . . .": Lear, *Witness*, 104.

"the world received . . .": Speech to Theta Sigma Phi, in Carson, *Lost Woods*, 150.

"I'd rather get . . .": Brooks, *The House of Life*, 71.

"Our enjoyment of . . .": Brooks, *The House of Life*, 72.

"a bit of seaweed . . . its own accord.": Brooks, *The House of Life*, 73–74. The full piece is reprinted in Brooks, 72–74.

"while it is . . .": Lear, *Witness*, 112.

"lively reading" and "one of the . . .": Brooks, *The House of Life*, 75.

"fastest small bird . . .": Carson, *Lost Woods*, 27.

"Not only does . . .": Carson, *Lost Woods*, 25.

"Observers have sometimes . . .": Carson, *Lost Woods*, 27.

"'I'm definitely in . . .": Brooks, *The House of Life*, 75–76.

CHAPTER SEVEN

"intransigent official ways . . . that gathering." "shoddy . . . absurd . . . field mice for twelve." and "we had almost . . .": Brooks, *The House of Life*, 78.

"an astonishing number . . .": Lear, *Witness*, 124.

"the whole delicate . . .": Carson letter to *Reader's Digest*, in Lear, *Witness*, 119.

"success" and "war": Lear, *Witness* has a brief summary of the typical press coverage, 119–120.

"It is really . . .": Lear, *Witness*, 131.

"wildlife resources of . . . essential environment.": U.S. Fish and Wildlife Service, *Conservation in Action*, "Guarding our Wildlife Resources" #5, 1.

"We presented quite . . .": Shirley Briggs's recollections, Lear, *Witness*, 133.

"Of course I'd . . .": Brooks, *The House of Life*, 101.

"an extra-long . . .": Lear, *Witness*, 142.

"The name 'whistling . . .": U.S. Fish and Wildlife Service, *Conservation in Action*, "Mattamuskeet" #4, 4.

"they would pass . . .": Lear, *Witness*, 140.

"The only reason . . .": Lear, *Witness*, 136.

"She was a very . . . shoddy behavior.": Sterling, *Sea and Earth*, 111.

"an inaccurate and . . .": Brooks, *The House of Life*, 77.

"We'd better fix . . .": Sterling, *Sea and Earth*, 112.

"ideal existence . . . do nothing.": Lear, *Witness*, 130.

CHAPTER EIGHT

"is that I . . .": Lear, *Witness*, 155.

"are ephemeral, created . . .": Carson, *The Sea Around Us*, 83.

"not much more . . .": Lear, *Witness*, 156.

*On August 27, 1883, Krakatoa, an island between Java and Sumatra, exploded in volcanic eruptions and disappeared.

"the next time . . .": Lear, *Witness*, 160.

"I am no . . .": Lear, Witness, 164–65.

"few better vehicles . . . forbidding shores": Brooks, *The House of Life*, 7.

"be sure of . . .": Lear, *Witness*, 162.

"How exquisitely delicate . . .": Brooks, *The House of Life*, 114.

"the difference between . . .": Letter to William Beebe, August 26, 1949, in Lear, *Witness*, 169.

"I was a Chaperone . . .": Carson, *Lost Woods*, 152.

"Surely we had . . . sleepy to bother": Carson, *Lost Woods*, 152–53.

"I think that . . .": Carson, *Lost Woods*, 153–54.

"I feel now . . ." and "a single morning . . .": Brooks, *The House of Life*, 119.

"Return to the Sea . . . at Sea.": Lear, *Witness*, 174.

"We have made . . .": Lear, *Witness*, 176.

"I am still . . .": Lear, *Witness*, 177.

"bold and starkly . . .": Brooks, *The House of Life*, 124.

"Heavens, is this . . .": Lear, *Witness*, 201.

"I grow more . . .": Lear, *Witness*, 199.

"the proprietor came . . .": Brooks, *The House of Life*, 131.

"The winds, the . . .": Carson, *Lost Woods*, 91.

"Most . . . say that . . . need of us.": Brooks, *The House of Life*, 129.

"Among male readers . . . reverse his convictions.": Brooks, *The House of Life*, 132.

"It's a pity . . .": *New York Times Book Review*, July 1, 1951, 1.

*One wonders how often a review of a book by a male writer talks about that writer's hair color and style, overall body type, eye color, or degree of masculinity.

"You are such . . .": Brooks, *The House of Life*, 132.

"Rachel as her readers . . ." and "'Oh,' Mrs. Carson . . .": Lear, *Witness*, 207.

"We live in . . .": National Book Award acceptance speech, in Carson, *Lost Woods*, 91.

"the amount of . . .": Lear, *Witness*, 203.

"The slender, gentle . . .": *New York Times*, Sunday April 27, 1952, 1.

"I am always . . .": Lear, *Witness*, 287.

"unaware that this . . . and for all.": Brooks, *The House of Life*, 152.

"The shore is . . .": Carson, *The Edge of the Sea*, 2.

CHAPTER NINE

"All that followed . . .": Freeman, *Always, Rachel*, 148.

"To do even . . .": Lear, 225.

"Scientists are often . . .": Lear, *Witness*, 224.

"Mankind has gone . . .": Lear, *Witness*, 221.

"as the most . . ." and "but *how* is . . .": Brooks, *The House of Life*, 9.

"Ecstatic!": Lear, *Witness*, 233.

"suggest that the . . . exploitation and destruction": Carson, *Lost Woods*, 99–100.

"the care of . . .": Lear, *Witness*, 238.

"Frankly, I could . . ." and "The practice of . . .": Lear, *Witness*, 239.

"The writer must . . .": Acceptance speech, American Association of University Women Achievement Award, June 22, 1956, in Brooks, *The House of Life*, 1–2.

"The heart of it . . .": Freeman, *Always, Rachel*, 28.

"to write the . . .": Brooks, *The House of Life*, 158.

"The place overlooks . . .": Lear, *Witness*, 235.

"Kindred spirit": Freeman, *Always, Rachel*, 23.

*Some readers find in Rachel and Dorothy Freeman's correspondence evidence of a lesbian relationship. I think it unlikely. Rachel's thinking and style of life makes it hard to believe she would have compromised (and I believe she would have seen it that way) her friendship with either Dorothy or Stanley, or in any way come between the two of them. Rachel's attachment to Stanley, while not as emotional as the one with Dorothy, meant a great deal to her. Stanley also became an important male figure for Rachel's grandnephew, Roger.

Dorothy was a prodigious letter-writer. Her correspondence with schoolmates, carried on for decades, employed many of the same extravagant expressions of affection. These letters were described to me by Rachel's biographer, Linda Lear. Lear noted, "From an historian's point of view, those who just look at DF's letters to RC, have no context, and it's only when you put in the larger view DF's total female network that you can say there's no lesbian relationship here, but a dear, loving, and devoted friendship." Linda J. Lear, private correspondence with author, February 11, 2006; interview with Lear, February 9, 2006.

"A writer is . . .": Lear, *Witness*, 249.

"I must never . . .": Lear, *Witness*, 533 n. 5.

"A stranger who . . .": Audubon Society lecture, December 13, 1954, in Brooks, *The House of Life*, 157.

"There is one . . .": Carson, *Lost Woods*, 159.

"I am not . . ." Carson, *Lost Woods*, 160.

"But I believe . . ." Carson, *Lost Woods*, 163.

"She's done it . . .": Lear, *Witness*, 262.

"What a wonderful . . . *The Sea Around Us*": Lear, *Witness*, 268.

"I am telling . . .": Brooks, *The House of Life*, 151.

"When the ebb . . .": Audubon Society Lecture, December 13, 1954, in Brooks, *The House of Life*, 159.

"people are fascinated . . .": Lear, *Witness*, 273.

"To understand the . . .": Carson, *The Edge of the Sea*, vii–viii.

"The main news . . .": *New York Times*, October 26, 1955, 17.

CHAPTER TEN

"a luxury just . . .": Freeman, *Always, Rachel*, 138.

"I am really . . . ferment of ideas.": Freeman, *Always, Rachel*, 145.

"Will you please . . .": Lear, *Witness*, 539 n. 40.

"Hidden in the . . .": A portion of the script is reprinted in Brooks, *The House of Life*, 198–99.

"The *Companion* editors . . .": Brooks, *The House of Life*, 200–201.

*A year after her death, *The Sense of Wonder* was published and has been reprinted in several editions.

"I have, as . . .": Brooks, *The House of Life*, 204.

"boggy ground . . . do about God?": Brooks, *The House of Life*, 206.

"I had been . . .": Lear, *Witness*, 287.

"lonely occupation at . . . a little frightening": Lear, *Witness*, 286.

"What is needed . . .": Freeman, *Always, Rachel*, 151.

"When, a few . . .": Brooks, *The House of Life*, 210.

*phosphorescence: These flashes near the shore on a dark night are made by millions of creatures part-plant and part-animal called dinoflagellates. The light is produced by chemical reactions that do not involve heat.

"He was flying . . .": Brooks, *The House of Life*, 208.

"The observation is . . . from your experience.": Brooks, *The House of Life* 208.

"lively as 17 . . ." and "We recalled our . . .": Lear, *Witness*, 300.

"The possibility of . . .": Freeman, *Always, Rachel*, 215.

"He had lost . . .": Brooks, *The House of Life*, 213.

"Not often in . . .": Freeman, *Always, Rachel*, 223.

"What a strange . . .": Freeman, *Always, Rachel*, 233.

"unattractive . . . am to write": Freeman, *Always, Rachel*, 248–49.

"In every outthrust . . .": *Holiday*, July 1958, reprinted in Brooks, *The House of Life*, 216–226.

"For all one . . .": Brooks, *The House of Life*, 220–21.

"Instead, they have . . .": Brooks, *The House of Life*, 225.

"Somewhere we should . . .": Brooks, *The House of Life*, 226.

"the cure for . . .": Lear, "Bombshell in Beltsville: The USDA and the Challenge of 'Silent Spring,'" *Agricultural History*, 66, 2, spring 1992, 157.

"died horribly": Brooks reprints Huckins's letter in full, *The House of Life*, 231–32.

"brought my attention . . .": Carson, *Silent Spring*, Acknowledgments.

CHAPTER ELEVEN

"After all, there . . .": Freeman, *Always, Rachel*, 257.

"It should cause . . .": Lear, *Witness*, 330.

"Knowing what I . . .": Freeman, *Always, Rachel*, 259.

"good allies, and . . .": Lear, *Witness*, 332.

"a psychological angle . . .": Brooks, *The House of Life*, 241.

"to build up . . .": Lear, *Witness*, 333.

"During that last . . . to heaven.": Freeman, *Always, Rachel*, 273.

"More than anyone . . .": Lear, *Witness*, 338.

"half baked, at . . .": Brooks, *The House of Life*, 243–44.

"I may seem . . .": Lear, *Witness*, 553 n.11.

"'an amazing rain . . . our own?": *Washington Post*, April 10, 1959, A12.

"We did not . . .": Brooks, *The House of Life*, 256.

"U.S. Is Losing . . .": *New York Times*, September 13, 1958, 1.

"Oh dear—his . . .": Freeman, *Always, Rachel*, 291.

"I know it . . .": Lear, *Witness*, 362.

"This may well . . .": Freeman, *Always, Rachel*, 280.

"So now I . . .": Lear, *Witness*, 364.

"I suppose it's . . .": Lear, *Witness*, 367.

"He should be" and "It was not . . .": Lear, *Witness*, 370.

"I do know . . .": Lear, *Witness*, 371.

"copies of letters . . .": Murphy, *What a Book*, 33.

*William O. Douglas dissented: *Murphy v. Butler*, 362 U.S. 929, March 28, 1960.

"I want to . . ." and "Dr. Sanderson did . . .": Lear, *Witness*, 379.

"I was told . . .": Lear, *Witness*, 368.

"I appreciate your . . .": Lear, *Witness*, 380.

"a deepened awareness . . . possible with him": Freeman, *Always, Rachel*, 332.

"so indescribably weak . . .": Freeman, *Always, Rachel*, 337.

"All these reminders . . .": Freeman, *Always, Rachel*, 355.

"The War Against Nature . . . Opus #4.": Lear, *Witness*, 386.

"how to reveal . . .": Freeman, *Always, Rachel*, 387.

"in the heart . . . all shall know.": Carson, *Silent Spring*, 1–3.

"Yes, there is . . .": Freeman, *Always, Rachel*, 390.

"But now that . . .": Freeman, *Always, Rachel*, 391.

"The calm courage . . .": Brooks, *The House of Life*, 265.

"'This is William . . .'" and "You know I have . . .": Freeman, *Always, Rachel*, 394.

CHAPTER TWELVE

"I want to . . .": Lear, *Witness*, 401.

"if only I . . .": Freeman, *Always, Rachel*, 400.

"rather mercurial . . . After . . .": Freeman, *Always, Rachel*, 401.

"I'm in luck . . .": Freeman, *Always, Rachel*, 403.

"Phenomenal!": *Saturday Review*, September 29, 1962, 18.

"few will read . . . from their test tubes.": *New York Times* editorial, July 2, 1962.

"'Heroine' of FDA . . .": *Washington Post*, July 15, 1962, A1.

"It is all . . .": Lear, *Witness*, 412.

"'Silent Spring' Is . . . a noisy fall": *New York Times*, July 22, 1962, F1.

"giant chemical companies . . . and sue": Quoted in the obituary for "Milton Greenstein," *New Yorker*, August 19, 1991, 79.

"Miss Carson presents . . .": *New York Times Book Review*, September 23, 1962, 26.

Silent Spring reached even more readers when Consumer's Union, publisher of *Consumer Reports* magazine, bought 40,000 copies to sell to its subscribers.

"The history of . . .": Carson, *Silent Spring*, 5.

"The public must . . .": Carson, *Silent Spring*, 13

"the campus is . . .": Carson, *Silent Spring*, 107.

"Who has made . . .": Carson, *Silent Spring*, 127.

"but we should . . .": Carson, *Silent Spring*, 64.

"The 'control of . . .": Carson, *Silent Spring*, 297.

"find little error . . . balance of nature": *New York Times*, July 22, 1962, F11.

"a spinster. What's . . .": Carson, *Silent Spring*, 50.

"probably a Communist": Lear, *Witness*, 429.

"Miss Rachel Carson's . . .": Lear, *Witness*, 409. The letter was printed in the *New Yorker*'s 70th anniversary issue, February 20–27, 1995, 18.

"No time . . . unnecessary interruptions.": Lear, *Witness*, 429–430. "No time" is a direct quote from Carson; "sometimes envied male writers . . ." is Lear's description of Carson's full response.

"a shy, soft-spoken . . .": Howard, *LIFE*, 105.

"Those who heard . . .": Lear, *Witness*, 454.

"BOM will carry . . .": Freeman, *Always, Rachel*, 407.

"As you listen . . .": January, 1963, Carson, *Lost Woods*, 222.

"informed people . . . patently unsound.": "Pesticides," *Time*, 45.

"For them should . . .": Brooks, *The House of Life*, 18*.

"the sort . . . that . . .": Lear, *Witness*, 421.

"of course, since . . .": Presidential press conference, August 29, 1962. See Brooks, *The House of Life*, 305.

"baloney" and "Silence, Miss Carson": Lear, *Witness*, 433; Murphy, *What a Book*, 101.

"*Silent Spring*, which . . .": Lear, *Witness*, 462.

"unusually well informed . . .": Brooks, *The House of Life*, 255.

"So far I . . .": Lear, *Witness*, 420.

"Now, don't sell . . . along comes Rachel Carson.": These cartoons by James Stevenson, J.W. Taylor, and Herbert Goldberg, among others, are reprinted in Brooks, *The House of Life*, insert after p. 238 and Lear, *Witness*, insert after p. 366.

"My text this . . . of it heartily.'": Lear, *Witness*, 426.

"will not be . . .": Lear, *Witness*, 336.

"no longer allows . . . parts per million": *House of Lords Debates*, March 20, 1963, 1134, quoted in Brooks, *The House of Life*, 312.

"What she wrote . . .": *CBS Reports*, April 3, 1963, transcript, 1.

"I just hope . . .": Freeman, *Always, Rachel*, 451.

"In a single . . .": Lear, *Witness*, 450.

"vindicated": *CBS Reports*, May 15, 1963, transcript, 27.

"Miss Rachel Carson . . .": *CBS Reports*, May 15, 1963, transcript, 31.

EPILOGUE

"But most of all . . .": Freeman, *Always, Rachel*, 467–68.

"So many ironic . . .": Freeman, *Always, Rachel*, 440.

"For exactly three . . .": Freeman, *Always, Rachel*, 504.

"would undertake to . . .": Lear, *Witness*, 477.

"Today we mourn . . .": Lear, *Witness*, 485.

"exhaustively researched, carefully . . ." and "such relatively rare . . .": U.S. Environmental Protection Agency, www.epa.gov/history/topics/epa/15c.htm.

"Then, pail and . . .": Brooks, *The House of Life*, 8.

Bibliography

Much has been written about Rachel Carson, from picture books to adult biographies and academic treatises. My list is eclectic, limited by space considerations, and is composed of books I found useful, ones Rachel Carson loved, and those one can dip into to begin to experience Rachel's world of nature.

Berrill, N.J., and Jacquelyn Berrill. *1001 Questions Answered About the Seashore*. New York: Dover, 1976. Covers questions most frequently asked about the seashore (tides, seaweeds, etc.) and about shore animals (squid, sea spiders, etc.).

Beston, Henry. *The Outermost House: A Year of Life on the Great Beach of Cape Cod* (1924). New York: Henry Holt and Co., 1949. A Carson favorite and a classic in nature writing. Beston spent a year alone in a tiny cottage, living with the rhythms of sea and sky.

Brooks, Paul. *The House of Life: Rachel Carson at Work*. Boston: Houghton Mifflin, 1972. A wonderful biography of a writer's life, enriched with selections from Carson's writings.

Carson, Rachel. *The Edge of the Sea*. Boston: Houghton Mifflin Co., 1955.

———. *Lost Woods: The Discovered Writing of Rachel Carson*. Linda Lear, ed. Boston: Beacon Press, 1998. A collection of childhood writings, essays, letters, speeches, and magazine articles.

Carson, Rachel L. *The Sea Around Us*. New York: Oxford University Press, 1951.

———. *The Sense of Wonder*. New York: Harper & Row, 1965.

———. *Silent Spring*. Boston: Houghton Mifflin Co., 1962.

———. *Under the Sea-Wind: A Naturalist's Picture of Ocean Life*. New York: Simon & Schuster, 1941.

Carson, R. L. "Undersea," *Atlantic Monthly*, September 1937.

CBS REPORTS. "The Silent Spring of Rachel Carson." Columbia Broadcasting System, Inc., April 13, 1963.

———. "The Verdict on the Silent Spring of Rachel Carson." Columbia Broadcasting System, Inc., May 15, 1963.

Crisler, Lois. *Arctic Wild*. New York: Harper & Row, 1958. A gripping account of eighteen months living, literally, with wolves and observing caribou and grizzlies in Alaska's Brooks Range. A book Carson thought was splendid.

Freeman, Martha, ed. *Always, Rachel: The Letters of Rachel Carson and Dorothy Freeman.* Boston: Beacon Press, 1995. A collection that offers a personal look at Carson.

Govan, Ada Clapham. *Wings at My Window.* New York: MacMillan, 1940. A true story of how a chickadee, singing on a bleak winter day, turned Govan into an ornithologist.

Graham, Frank Jr. *Since Silent Spring.* Boston: Houghton Mifflin Co., 1970. An excellent look at the controversy *Silent Spring* provoked, a review of Carson's evidence, and a look at the beginnings of the environmental movement her work inspired.

Harlan, Judith. *Sounding the Alarm: A Biography of Rachel Carson.* Minneapolis: Dillon Press, 1989. A fine middle-grade biography.

Harvey, Mary Kersey. "Using a Plague to Fight a Plague: The Author," *Saturday Review,* September 29, 1962.

Howard, Jane. "The Gentle Storm Center," *LIFE,* October 12, 1962.

The Lear/Carson Collection. Department of Special Collections and Archives, Charles E. Shain Library, Connecticut College, www.conncoll.edu/is/info-resources/special-collections/learcarson.htm. Primary and secondary materials relating to the life, work, and achievement of Rachel Carson, given to Connecticut College in 1998 by environmental historian Linda Lear, author of *Rachel Carson: Witness for Nature.*

Lear, Linda. "Bombshell in Beltsville: The USDA and the Challenge of 'Silent Spring,'" *Agricultural History*, 66, 2, spring 1992, p. 157

——. *Rachel Carson: Witness for Nature*. New York: Henry Holt, 1997. Detailed and fascinating, often riveting. Lear, Carson's preeminent biographer, uncovered new materials, and has established the Lear/Carson Collection at Connecticut College.

Leonard, Jonathan Norton. "And His Wonders in the Deep," *New York Times Books Review*, July 1, 1951.

Lynch, Jim. *The Highest Tide*. New York: Bloomsbury, 2005. Coming-of-age novel about a thirteen-year-old boy who lives by the shore and is devoted to Carson's work.

Matthiessen, Peter. "Environmentalist: Rachel Carson," *Time*, March 29, 1999.

Milne, Lorus, and Margery Milne. "There's Poison All Around Us Now," *New York Times Book Review*, September 23, 1962.

"Milton Greenstein," *New Yorker*, August 19, 1991.

Murphy, Priscilla Coit. *What a Book Can Do: The Publication and Reception of Silent Spring*. Amherst: University of Massachusetts Press, 2005. Academic study of how newspapers, magazines, and publishing dealt with the phenomenon of *Silent Spring*.

"Pesticides: The Price for Progress," *Time*, September 28, 1962.

The Rachel Carson Collection. Archives, Chatham College, Pittsburgh, PA., www.chatham.edu/host/library/Carson/index.html. The Collection includes short stories, essays, and newspaper articles written by Rachel Carson during her studies at the Pennsylvania College for Women, as well as her photographs and correspondence. The collection also includes secondary source information as well as a series of materials relating to the Rachel Carson Institute.

Sterling, Philip. *Sea and Earth: The Life of Rachel Carson*. New York: Thomas Y. Crowell Co., 1970. One of the first biographies of Carson for young readers. Sterling interviewed family and friends who tell engaging but sometimes inaccurate stories. No sources cited.

U.S. Fish and Wildlife Service, Department of the Interior. *Conservation in Action*. Washington, D.C.: Government Printing Office, 1948. Series edited by Carson. Carson's booklets can be downloaded from www.fws.gov.

Wadsworth, Ginger. *Rachel Carson: Voice for the Earth*. Minneapolis: Lerner, 1992. Fine biography for young readers.

ADDITIONAL SITES:
Rachel Carson Web page: www.rachelcarson.org. Established by Carson's biographer Linda Lear and devoted to the life and legacy

of Rachel Carson. A site rich in links to current news, books, and articles by and about Carson, additional sources, conferences, etc.

Rachel Carson Council, Inc. RCC, Inc. P.O. Box 10779, Silver Spring, MD 20914, 301-593-7507. http://members.aol.com/rccouncil/about_us. Clearinghouse and library of materials on pesticide-related issues. Housed in Carson's last home.

Rachel Carson Homestead: National Historic Site. 613 Marion Avenue, Box 46, Springdale, PA 15144, 724-274-5459; www.rachelcarsonhomestead.org. Educational programs on the environment. Housed in Carson's childhood home.

Rachel Carson National Wildlife Refuge. www.fws.gov/northeast/rachelcarson. 207-646-9229. Fifty miles of coastline in York and Cumberland counties, Maine. Homepage with a great deal of material. The Web site also includes samples of Carson's writings.

Environmental Research Foundation. www.rachel.org

The Science and Environmental Health Network. www.sehn.org

Beyond Pesticides. www.beyondpesticides.org

Pesticide Action Network of North America. www.panna.org

U.S. Environmental Protection Agency. www.epa.gov

Permissons and Acknowledgments

THE AUTHOR IS grateful for permission to quote material from the following sources: all Rachel Carson writings published in *Always, Rachel: The Letters of Rachel Carson and Dorothy Freeman*, ed. Martha Freeman (Boston: Beacon Press, 1995); *The House of Life: Rachel Carson at Work*, Paul Brooks (Boston: Houghton Mifflin, 1972); *Lost Woods: The Discovered Writing of Rachel Carson*, ed. Linda Lear (Boston: Beacon Press, 1998); *Rachel Carson: Witness for Nature*, Linda Lear (New York: Henry Holt, 1997); from Rachel Carson's books, *The Edge of the Sea*, *The Sea Around Us*, *Silent Spring*, and *Under the Sea-Wind*; and unpublished materials courtesy of the Lear/Carson Collection, Connecticut College, and the Rachel Carson Collection, Chatham College, reprinted by permission of Frances Collin, Trustee. In addition, other materials are reprinted with permission from *The House of Life*, Paul Brooks (Boston: Houghton

Mifflin, 1972); the Lear/Carson Collection, Connecticut College; and the Rachel Carson Collection, Chatham College, Pittsburgh, Pennsylvania.

I am most beholden to Tracy Gates for her commitment, enthusiasm, and editing skills; I'm also very grateful for all the help of the editorial, art, and production staffs of Viking Children's Books. And a special thanks to Jill Davis, with whom this project began.

I am indebted to the following people (affiliations for identification purposes only): Jay Bellanca, Miriam Cohen, Aaron Colangelo (NRDC), Frances Collin (Frances Collin, Literary Agent, Trustee), Peg Culver (Bancroft Public Library), Ann Diamond, Dr. Stanley Freeman, Judith Hole (CBS), Ruth Ihne, Dr. Diana Post (Rachel Carson Council), Peter Sauer, Dr. Irma Smith (Chatham College), Jane Spinak (Columbia University School of Law), Sarah Yake (Frances Collin Literary Agency), Rhonda Yeager (Chatham College); and, for their unwavering support, my New York writers group and dear friends from Vermont College. Very special thanks to Dr. Linda Lear (Professor of Environmental History, George Washington University) and Laurie Deredita (Curator, Special Collections, Connecticut College) for their most generous support.

PHOTO CREDITS

Pages 10 (photo by Shirley Briggs), 14 (Carson family photo), 35, 55 (photo by Mary Frye), 95 (sketches by Shirley Briggs), 104 (photo by Shirley Briggs), 180: courtesy The Lear/Carson Collection, Connecticut College.

Pages 32, 66: the Yale Collection of American Literature, Beinecke Rare Book and Manuscript Library, Yale University, courtesy The Lear/Carson Collection, Connecticut College.

Pages 42, 50: courtesy Rachel Carson Collection, Archives, Chatham College, Pittsburgh, Pennsylvania.

Page 80: courtesy the Yale Collection of American Literature, Beinecke Rare Book and Manuscript Library, Yale University.

Page 122: courtesy U.S. Fish and Wildlife Service.

Pages 127, 138, 186: courtesy Freeman Family Collection.

Page 154: July 8, 1945, Jones Beach State Park, N.Y. © Bettmann/Corbis.

Front cover: Alfred Eisenstaedt/Time & Life Pictures/Getty Images.

Back cover: photo by Shirley Briggs, courtesy The Lear/Carson Collection, Connecticut College.

Index

Page numbers in italics refer to captions or illustrations.